Cakes

For All Occasions

Geraldine Kidwell

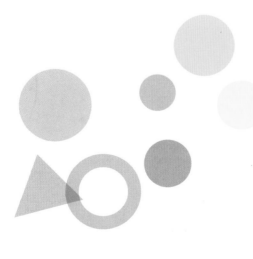

4880 Lower Valley Road Atglen, Pennsylvania 19310

Schiffer Books are available at special discounts for bulk purchases for sales pro-motions or premiums. Special editions, including personalized covers, corporate imprints, and excerpts can be created in large quantities for special needs. For more information contact the publisher:

Published by Schiffer Publishing Ltd.
4880 Lower Valley Road
Atglen, PA 19310
Phone: (610) 593-1777; Fax: (610) 593-2002
E-mail: Info@schifferbooks.com

For the largest selection of fine reference books on this and related subjects, please visit our web site at **www.schifferbooks.com**
We are always looking for people to write books on new and related subjects. If you have an idea for a book please contact us at the above address.

This book may be purchased from the publisher.
Include $3.95 for shipping.
Please try your bookstore first.
You may write for a free catalog.

In Europe, Schiffer books are distributed by
Bushwood Books
6 Marksbury Ave.
Kew Gardens
Surrey TW9 4JF England
Phone: 44 (0) 20 8392-8585; Fax: 44 (0) 20 8392-9876
E-mail: info@bushwoodbooks.co.uk
Website: www.bushwoodbooks.co.uk
Free postage in the U.K., Europe; air mail at cost.

Designed by RoS
Type set in Zurich BT

ISBN: 978-0-7643-2904-3
Printed in China

Dedication

I would like to take this opportunity to recognize my family who vigorously support my sugar art even when it takes time away from them. Thanks to my husband Bill, our children, Bret, Gina and Lori, our grandchildren, Bretani, Collan, Hunter, and Wesley and my mother Gladys. Each of these individuals contributes to my endeavors and to the person I am.

Thanks to my special and close friends who are involved in the world of sugar art. Leigh Sipe, Darlene Nold, Cindy Hall and Sam and Elaine Stringer have each contributed in their own special way from support and encouragement, gathering supplies, proof reading skills and taking outstanding photographs. I could not have completed this task without all of you.

In addition, I would like to dedicate this "how to" book to the young and beginning decorators. The future of sugar art rests in your hands. Never let anyone discourage you because you use a different method to achieve a desired result. That is how new techniques are born. Work hard, continue learning and do not give up because you have a problem. Explore cake clubs and organizations such as I.C.E.S. (International Cake Exploration Societe www.ices.org) for demonstrations, classes and new ideas. Perseverance always pays in the end. Offer your customers the same qualities that you would expect of a professional such as individualism, imagination and quality ingredients for a creative confection. Remember, you are the next generation of sugar artists.

Introductions

It is my pleasure to introduce you to Geraldine Kidwell. Geraldine is a master decorator from the Louisville, Kentucky, area. She has competed in many major shows and taught classes to decorators around the world. Most importantly, she has inspired people everywhere to do their best and to think positively. Thank you Geraldine, you have always been a dear friend to me as well as my mentor.

Linda Shonk
Choco-Pan
Indianapolis, Indiana
www.chocopan.com

It is my privilege to introduce Geraldine Kidwell of Artistry In Cake of Kentucky. Geraldine is a true professional leader in the wedding industry. The combination of her delicious cakes and artistic sugar art is something that should be sought after by brides and professionals alike. She is someone that leads by example and is willing to explain and teach her art to various students who are interested in her skills. It has been a great pleasure to call her my friend and professional mentor. Thank you Geraldine for the example you set among other professionals in today's wedding industry. You should be proud of the accomplishments you have achieved in cake artistry. You will always be an award winner to me.

Tammy Sharp
Chaney's Chocolates
www.chaneyschocolates.com

Introduction

Welcome to the wonderful world of sugar art. If you have had a course in basic decorating and are currently wondering what should be the next step in your education, then this is the book for you. You will be able to explore different frosting media, types of cake boards and frames, sculpted cakes, purchased as well as household items for tools, designs for different occasions, and numerous ideas for life's occasions celebrations. Cake decorating is an incredible method of artistic expression that can be shared by every part of our society, whether male or female, young or old, novice or professional. This book is targeted for the decorator who has taken basic decorating classes and is looking for a more advanced area to explore and expand their talents. The text covers a wide range of cakes, from the basic cake that can be decorated with candies without the use of a decorator tip, to ice cream and gum ball characters, to an elegant tier wedding cake accented with fondant.

The intent of the book is to introduce you to various frosting media and the incorporation and blending of them. A buttercream cake can take on the appearance of an illustration from an elegant magazine article with proper smoothing and the addition of a few fondant drapes or flowers. The flavor of fondant can be enhanced by blending it with white chocolate or flavorings. Rolled buttercream can become more stable when blended with half fondant. Royal icing can be used for accents on buttercream to prevent bleeding of dark colors. The mingling of various frostings can produce incredible results. Do not feel restricted to one. When decorating the cakes in this book, feel free to substitute one frosting for another.

Unless otherwise stated, all cakes are baked in 2-inch deep pans and most included cake boards are 1/2-inch thick plywood with a matching satin ribbon glued to the edge. Do not limit your scope of possibilities, but explore and experiment with new as well as established ideas. Have fun with the art. What other hobby could you have where you could eat your mistakes?

Contents

Chapter 1

Celebrating
A New Baby

. . . .

Special Delivery

The birth of a baby is usually the first of many occasions when people search for a special cake to aid in the celebration of life. Whether you choose a simple undecorated white cake with colored frosting or copy the picture on the birth announcement or a party napkin, the cake is the focal point of the party and always signifies a happy occasion.

Supplies
- 1 covered cake board, 14-inch x 20-inch
- 1 half sheet cake, 12-inch x 18-inch x 2-inch
- One 7-inch x 9-inch x 2-inch oval cake
- 1 large muffin
- 1 Twinkie or oblong snack cake
- Mold for small alphabet letters (CK Products)
- 1/2 pound fondant colored as described in text
- #67 decorator tip or equivalent large leaf tip
- Decorator star tip #21
- Buttercream frosting in pink, white and yellow
- Stork pattern (included in pattern section)
- Paper towel without pattern or design such as Viva brand
- 1 piece of foam core board, 12-inch x 10-inch, to form stork pattern

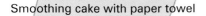

Smoothing cake with paper towel

Smooth frosted sheet cake

Bake and cool a half sheet cake. Cover the cake board with a grease proof covering such as foil, saran wrap over a design or contact paper, and center the cake on the covered board.

Frost the entire cake with soft pink buttercream frosting or the color of your choice. Allow the frosting to air dry until you can touch it and it feels dry and powdery. Place a design-free paper towel over the surface and rub it lightly with your hand to smooth the surface and edges. If you have a problem with finger prints showing on the cake through the towel, then rub over the paper towel with a cake smoother.

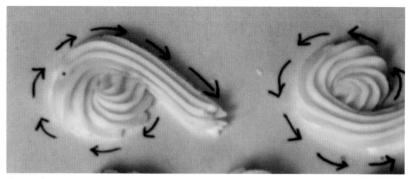

Steps for reverse shell

Reverse shell on sheet cake

Add a white or contrasting reverse shell border around the bottom edge of the cake with decorator tip #21. This pattern requires that you pipe the turn of one shell clockwise and the next shell counter clockwise so that every other shell is piped in the reverse direction.

Cake pieces of stork

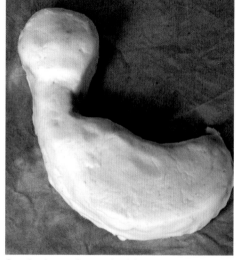

Stork pieces frosted white

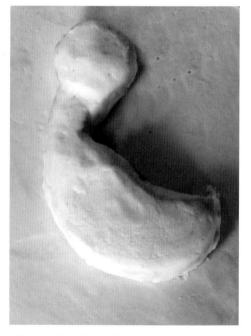

Stork placed on sheet cake

Lay the oval cake onto the stork pattern that has been pre-cut from a piece of foam core board or a regular cake board. Cut a section from the 7-inch oval cake to form the contour of the back and tail. Remove this section and position it in place for the neck of the stork. Place a large muffin in place for the head.

Frost the stork pieces with white buttercream. Add extra frosting and smooth it where the pieces fit together to form an invisible connection.

Use the paper towel to smooth the stork and gently pinch the frosting to form sharp, pointed, curved tail feathers.

Steps to trim Twinkie for beak

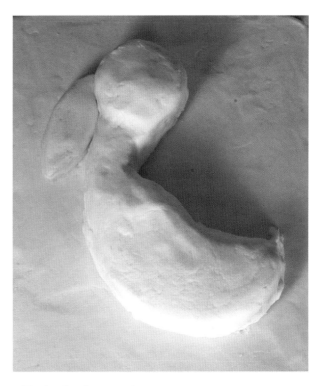

Placing beak on stork

Frosted yellow Twinkie beak

Unwrap a purchased, oblong snack cake, such as a Twinkie, and trim the lower end to a point to form the beak. Trim a piece from the top end so that it will fit snugly against the head.

Frost the beak completely with yellow buttercream and smooth it with a paper towel.

Position the beak against the head of the stork and secure it in place with frosting.

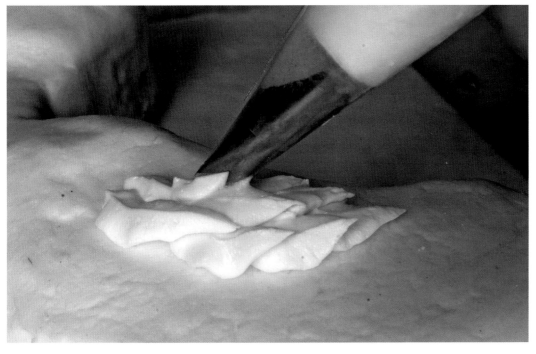

Place a #67 decorator leaf tip into a pastry bag and fill it with white buttercream frosting. Use the leaf tip to form overlapping rows of feathers on the wing and tail of the stork.

Piping wing feathers

To form the eye, use a pea size piece of black fondant. Flatten the piece slightly to form a small oval. Add a small oval of white fondant then place a smaller ball of blue or black for the pupil of the eye. Add the eye to the face and accent it with eyelashes, which are painted with black food color and a tiny paint brush.

Steps to form the eye

The hat can be formed from fondant, using black or the color of your choice. [A] Roll the fondant into a thin, round-shaped piece. Cut a circle with a cutter or rounded object such as a jar lid from a wide mouth jar. [B] Because the stork is two-dimensional and only part of the hat will be visible, you will need to cut about one third from one side of the hat circle. [C] Brush the back side of the hat lightly with piping gel or liquid, and position the hat over the top of the stork's head. Use the dull side of a table knife to mark the sections of the ball cap. Roll a pea-size ball of the same fondant, flatten and place it at the center top for the button on top of the hat. [D] Roll an oblong piece of fondant to cut the bill of the hat. Trim the bill to fit, then prop it and allow to dry until the piece will hold its shape when it is attached to the hat.

Steps for forming the hat

To form the legs, roll long, thin strips of yellow fondant that are approximately 5 inches long. Measure 4 inches from the top and slightly mark the ankle area. Flatten the lower 1 inch to form the foot. Cut each foot with small scissors to form three toes. Roll each toe to elongate and shape it. Position the legs at the lower edge of the stork body and attach with a little white fondant. Add a few white feathers with the #67 decorator tip.

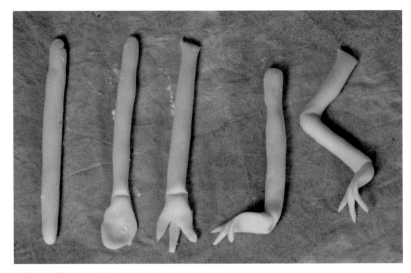

Steps for stork legs

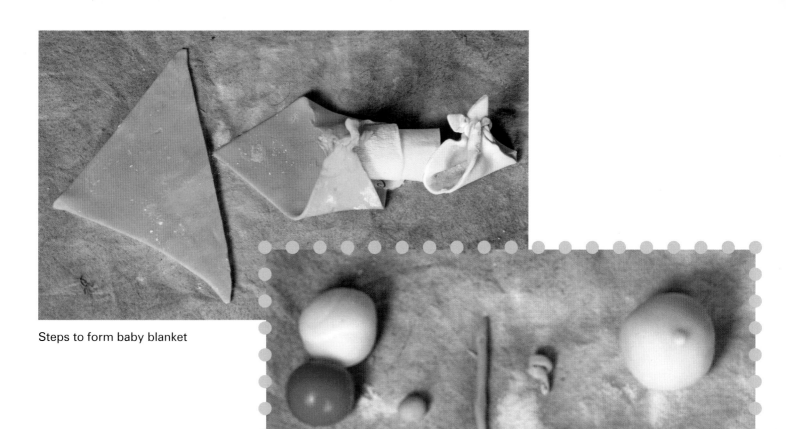

Steps to form baby blanket

Steps to form baby head

Thinly roll a piece of darker pink fondant and cut it into a triangle-shape that is about 3 inches at the widest point. Fold the three corners together and dampen slightly to attach. This will form an opening for the baby head. Place a small piece of paper towel into the opening to maintain the space until the fondant dries.

The body of the baby appears to be inside the blanket so it is only necessary to form the head. Use flesh-colored fondant to cover a gum ball. Flesh color for a Caucasian baby is best achieved with a slight touch of pink food color, light brown for an African-American baby, or the appropriate combination for other races. Roll it in the palm of your hand until it is perfectly smooth. Roll a tiny log of brown fondant around a toothpick to form a curl and attach it to the top of the head. Create the nose with a tiny ball of flesh-colored paste.

Remove the paper towel from the blanket and place the head into the opening. Secure it with a little frosting. Form the eyes with two dots of black or blue food color and a tiny brush. Place the blanket and baby into the beak of the stork.

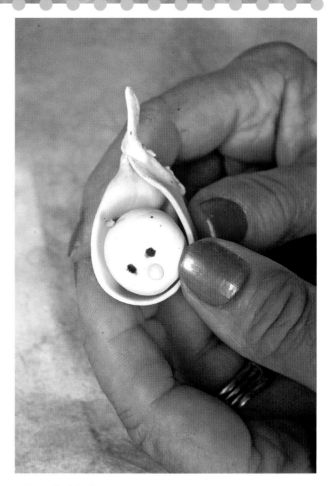

Baby in blanket

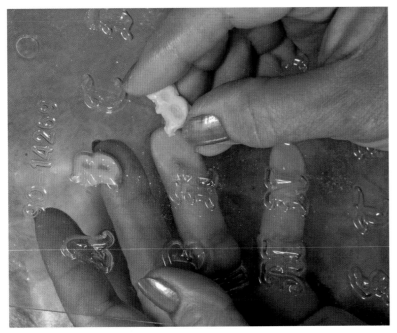

Molding letters in mold

Steps to form baby rattle

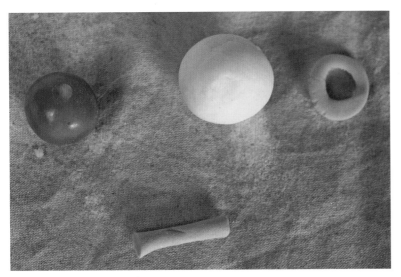

Completed baby rattle

A message can be added to the cake by using a plastic alphabet mold. Roll a very small piece of fondant into a thin oblong piece and place it into a letter. Use a large corsage pin to encourage the letter to release from the mold.

The baby rattles for the cake are optional but they add a little color and interest. They are formed in three pieces. For the ball of the rattle, use a tiny gum ball and roll it in a piece of pastel fondant. The handle is a very small log of a contrasting color. The handle is cut using the large open end of a decorator tip and the hole is cut with a #12 decorator tip. The individual pieces are more visible if you use contrasting colors.

Allow the pieces to dry and attach them with a tiny amount of royal frosting. Position the pieces at random areas on the cake and attach with frosting.

Sleeping Baby

Supplies
- Two 9-inch x 2-inch oval cake layers
- 1 cake board, 14-inch x 18-inch, covered
- 1 very large muffin
- 2-1/2 pounds fondant
- Buttercream frosting, color of baby sleeper and color of hair
- Small manicure scissors
- Baby face mold
- Decorator tips #5, 3, 12
- One decorator bag
- Baby pink dusting powder

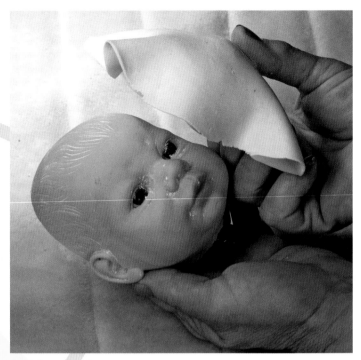

Doll face mold

If you are unable to find a suitable baby face mold, look at your local dollar store, discount toy shop, or your daughter's toy chest for an inexpensive baby doll. Should you want to keep your baby face for a permanent mold, remove the head and cut the face area from the doll. If you want to keep the toy intact, you can mold the face directly on the doll. Color a large ball of fondant that is big enough to form the face, hands, and feet. Use a light pink or flesh color to tint the paste.

Roll a golf ball-size piece of fondant into a thin sheet that is large enough to cover the face of your doll. You do not want this covering to be tissue thin, but it should be approximately the thickness of 3 or 4 sheets of typing paper laid together. Brush the back side of this piece with powdered sugar and lay it over the face of the doll.

Gently press the fondant into the crevasses of the facial features until the fondant forms a facial mask. Use a small pointed object such as a skewer or a toothpick to make the nostril and mouth openings. Mold only one ear onto the face because the baby is lying on the other side of his head and the second ear will not show. Most doll babies will have ears for you to mold as part of the face. Trim the mask around the hair line and leave it on the doll overnight to dry.

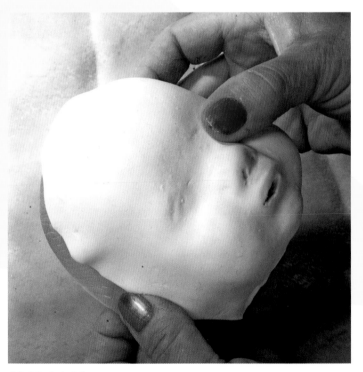

Molded doll face

Steps to form baby feet

Form two balls from the flesh-colored fondant for the feet. Each ball should be approximately the size of a golf ball. Keep the balls covered in a plastic bag while they are not in use, as they will dry quickly. Roll one ball until smooth.

Flatten the ball and form it into a slight wedge-shape foot that is narrow at the heel and wider at the toes.

Pinch up a small amount to form the heel and shape the ankle area so that it will fit into the leg opening of the baby sleeper.

Use the dull side of a table knife to mark creases for the joints of the toes and add additional character lines on the bottom of the foot.

With small manicure scissors, make four cuts for the toes. Lightly roll each toe between your thumb and forefinger to round the cut edges. Bend the toes slightly to create a realistic, normal movement of the foot. Repeat this procedure for the other foot. Make sure that you have a left and a right foot. Lay the feet top side down to dry as the soles of the feet will be up on the finished cake.

From the remaining flesh colored fondant, form two balls that are slightly smaller than the feet. Each ball will be about the size of a walnut. Roll the ball until it is smooth, then flatten it into an oval patty that is less than 1/4-inch thick.

Pinch slightly in the wrist area so that it will fit into the sleeve of the baby sleeper. Mark the finger joint areas with the dull side of a table knife as you did for the feet. A small ball tool or the rounded end of a small paint brush can be used to form the contour of the palm. Look at your own hand as a guide.

Use the manicure scissors to cut a pie shape wedge from the front of the hand and discard. This will divide the thumb from the other fingers. Make three equal cuts to create the four fingers. Roll and elongate each finger and the thumb slightly. Bend the fingers for a natural look. Usually the little finger is bent the most and each succeeding finger is bent a little less. Repeat the procedure for the other hand then prop each hand with pieces of soft paper towel to dry.

Baby hand

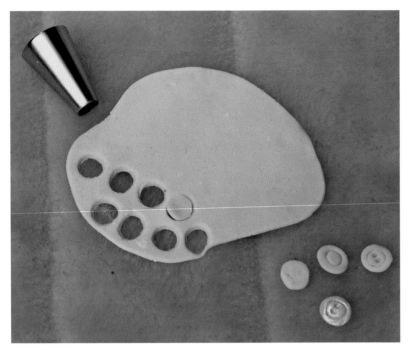

Steps to form buttons

To make the sleeper buttons, color a small ball of fondant the same shade as you plan to make the baby sleeper. Roll the ball out thinly. Use a #12 decorator tip to cut the buttons and flatten each slightly between your thumb and forefinger. Indent each button slightly with a #5 decorator tip to form a slightly smaller circle. Mark the button holes with the sharp tip of a small skewer. Allow the buttons to dry overnight, then brush each with pearl luster.

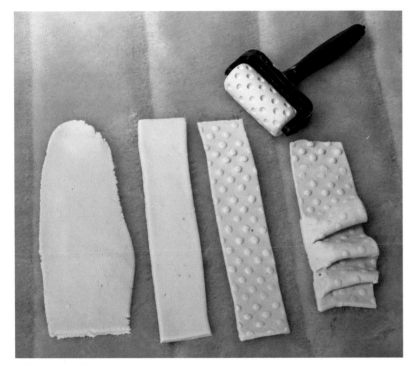

Ribbon ruffle steps

Frost a 14-inch x 18-inch cake board with buttercream or fondant frosting. Color a pound of fondant the same color as the baby sleeper. Roll a section of this fondant into a long oblong or log shape. Flatten the piece with a rolling pin until very thin.

Cut the ribbon into 1-1/2-inch strips using either a ribbon cutter or a pizza cutter. The ribbon can be left plain or embossed with numerous patterns created with embossing rollers.

Working from left to right, lift the ribbon and overlap it to the left to form a pleat. Continue this procedure for the full length of the strip. Roll the top of the pleated area to secure and trim it with the pizza cutter. Place this strip on the edge of the cake board and secure it with a small amount of frosting.

Repeat the process until the ribbon goes all the way around the board. Beading around the top of the ruffle is piped with a #5 decorator tip. If you need more cake than you feel the baby will serve, it can be placed on a half-sheet cake, using the ruffle to decorate the cake rather than the board.

Carving cake pieces

To form the baby, you will need two 9-inch oval cakes and one large muffin. Cut an oval cake board or foam core board that will hold a 9-inch oval and the baby head. If the baby is placed on this board, it will be easier to pick it up and move it onto the decorated board. Place the first oval on the cake board and frost the oval with buttercream frosting. Place the second oval on top of the first.

Using a serrated knife, start at the middle of the oval, which would be 4-1/2 inches from the end of the cake, and trim the front to a slant that forms the baby's shape. Remove this angled piece. If you feel that the rear of the baby sticks up high enough, you can dispose of this cut piece.

If you need more elevation on the rear then turn the cut piece around and place it on the rear of the baby cake. Trim all the edges to give them a rounded contour. Carve a wedge from the base of the bottom oval at the rear of the baby so that the little bottom cups under. Cut a piece from the one side of the head so that it fits firmly against the body and secure the head to the body with frosting.

Stacked oval cake

Moving carved front piece to back

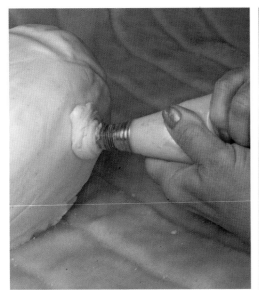
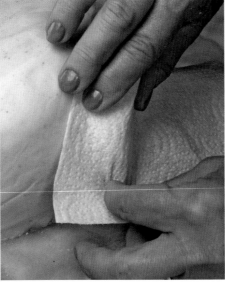

Piping arms and legs   Smoothing baby leg

Frost the baby body with blue frosting for the sleeper. Frost the face area with pink or white as it will be covered with the pre-made facial mask. Place a coupler into the decorator bag, but do not add a decorator tip. Fill the bag with blue frosting and pipe arms and legs. Pipe large, full legs that curve at the cake board for the knees and curve the arms at the elbow.

Let the frosting air dry slightly then cover the leg and rub with a non textured paper towel. This will smooth your frosting and eliminate all of the wrinkles and marks. Repeat this procedure for the second leg and both of the arms. Press the paper towel into the ends of the legs and sleeves to form an opening for the feet and hands.

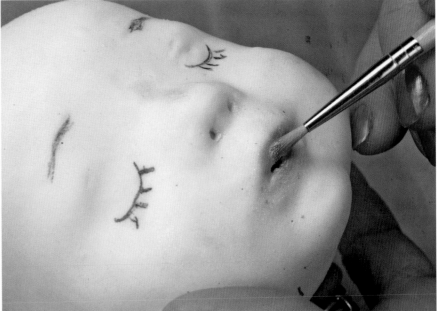

Painting facial mask

Inserting foot in sleeper

Insert the pre-made feet into the ends of the sleeper legs and attach them with a little frosting. Place the bottom of the feet facing up. Insert the hands into the ends of the sleeves and position the hands in a natural position.

Place the dried fondant facial mask onto the baby face and secure it with frosting. You will need to paint the facial features with a very small paint brush. Mix a small amount of brown gel paste color with white to soften the color. Lightly paint the eye brows and lashes on the closed eyes. Brush the lips with a light pink. Use the baby pink dusting powder and a Q-Tip to highlight the cheeks.

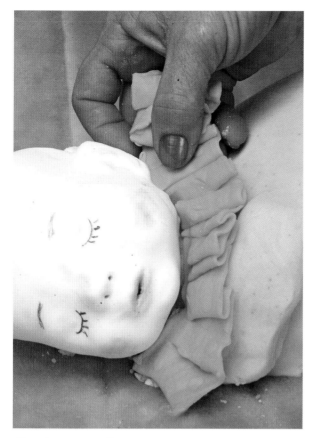

Forming neck ruffle

Place a 1-inch ruffle around the neck of the baby to conceal the facial connection. Form the ruffle as described under the ribbon ruffle that trimmed the board.

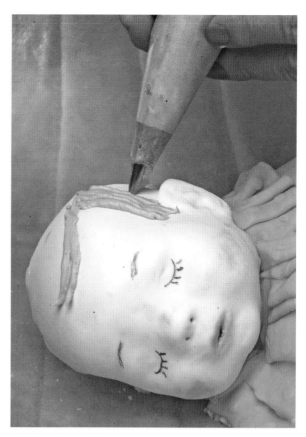

Piping baby hair

Use brown frosting, or your favorite hair color, to pipe hair for the baby with a #5 decorator tip. Keep the natural lines of hair in mind as you pipe the strands. If you are creating a baby girl, you might want to have more curls than for the little boy. Pat the hair slightly to blend it together.

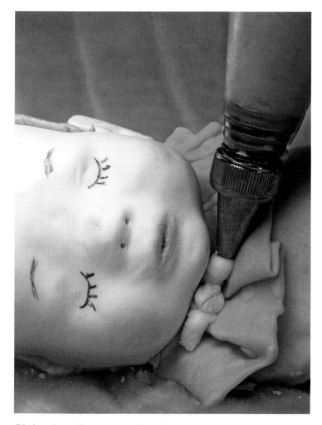

Piping beading around neck

Trim the ruffle with blue buttercream beading applied with a #5 decorator tip.

Using a rounded skewer or a small paint brush, press an indentation around the rear of the sleeper to represent a button up flap. Place the dried buttons around the flap and attach each with frosting at regular intervals.

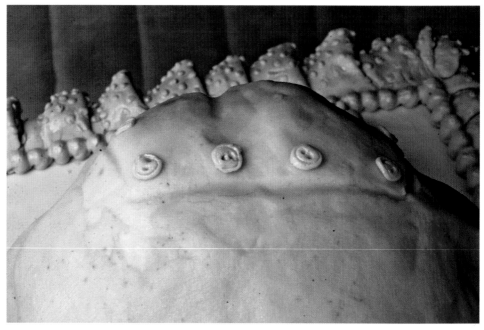

Buttons on flap

Steps for pacifier

To form the pacifier, roll a teardrop-shape nipple from pink fondant. The disk part is cut from the big end of a large decorator tube. The outer ring of the handle is cut using the large end of a regular size tip and the hole is cut using a #12 tip. Allow the pieces to dry before assembly. Attach the nipple to the flat disk so that the nipple is facing straight up.

When this part dries, attach the handle and place it in the baby's hand. If you prefer that the pacifier be in the baby's mouth, you can eliminate the nipple and attach the flat disk and handle directly to the mouth.

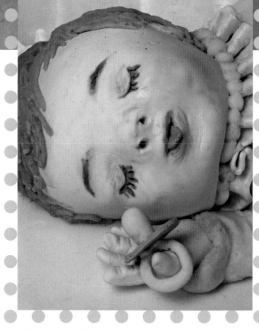

Close up of pacifier

Baby Attire

Girl's Dress

Supplies
- 1 quarter sheet cake, 9-inch x 13-inch x 2-inch, for dress or romper
- 12-inch x 15-inch cake board or cut to contour
- Buttercream frosting
- 2 pounds of rolled buttercream frosting (in recipe section)
- Golf ball-size piece of brown fondant for trim on romper
- 1/4 pound white fondant for softball pattern and dress lace
- 1/8 pound of green fondant for bodice lace
- Narrow lace impression mat
- Wide lace impression mat
- White pearl luster
- Small paint brush
- Pizza cutter

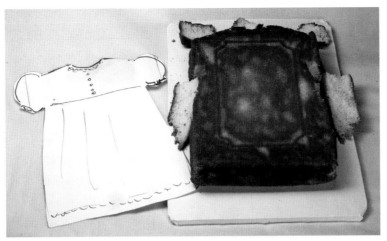

Carved cake

Crumb-coated dress cake

Cut a heavy cake board that is one inch larger than the contour of the pattern and cover it with a grease resistant covering. For both the dress and the romper use a one-quarter sheet cake pan. For a larger crowd, the same effect can be achieved with a half sheet cake. Trim the neck and shoulder area of the dress, using the pattern as a guide. Cut a section from under each arm to accent the sleeves. Use the discarded pieces of cake to shape and build up the sleeves.

Crumb coat the entire cake with buttercream. Build up the sleeve and other necessary areas with extra frosting for the best contour appearance.

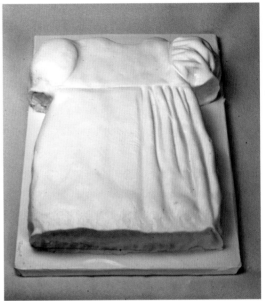

Dress covered with rolled buttercream

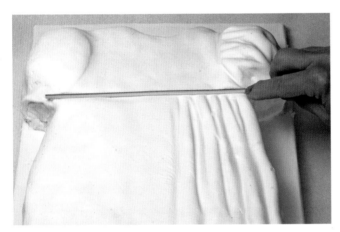

Marking bodice with skewer

Rolled buttercream is easier to handle if you roll it between two sheets of upholstery plastic or something similar. In this instance, I have rolled the frosting on a 12-inch x 17-inch plastic place mat. The frosting adheres to the mat and allows you to pick it up and invert it over the crumb-coated cake. When the frosting is centered over the cake you can gently pull off the mat and allow the frosting to fall onto the cake. Rolled buttercream is very conductive to the heat from your hands so you can easily rub folds and pleats with the high and low ridges of your frosting. Lightly push in indentations and smooth areas of the sleeve to create a 3D appearance to give the appearance of a sleeve hole.

Use a rounded object, such as a small wooden skewer, to mark the seam areas for the sleeves and yolk of the dress. If you have a baby outfit to copy it will help you with the placement of the seams. The bodice on the dress is perfectly smooth but the skirt is full and gathered below the yolk. Try to have numerous creases near the yolk and fewer and wider at the hem.

The sleeves should be very full and puffy with creases to represent the gathered fullness.

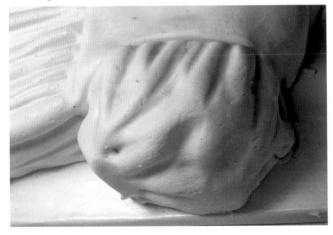

Fullness in sleeve

Lace mold and molded bodice lace

Rolls of lace on bodice

The cake pictured shows the use of lace impression mats to make rows of lace running vertically on the bodice. There are numerous companies that produce these molds so you can be creative and experiment with different molds. Roll a long thin piece of light green fondant or gum paste and press it firmly into the mold. Trim any excess that protrudes over the edge. With the aid of a corsage pin or a toothpick, loosen the lace from the mold at one end. Invert the mold and let the lace gently fall out.

Measure the distance from the shoulder to the bodice seam and place three rows of lace on either side of the center of the dress. Dip a tiny brush into a high alcohol content liquid, such as Vodka or pure lemon extract, and trace a line down the front of the bodice to secure the lace trim. Blot off any excess liquid with a paper towel. A liquid with a high alcoholic content will dampen the area, but the alcohol quickly evaporates to leave a dry area. Water would make the fondant sticky.

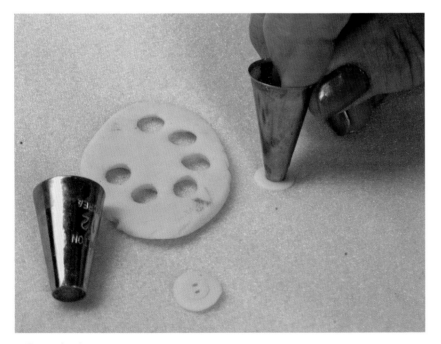

Steps for buttons

Roll out a small piece of fondant and cut five circles with a #12 decorator tip for the buttons. Mark inside the circle with a #5 decorator tip to form a circular impression. Use a toothpick to mark two holes in each bottom and place the five buttons on the center front of the bodice, securing them with a touch of frosting.

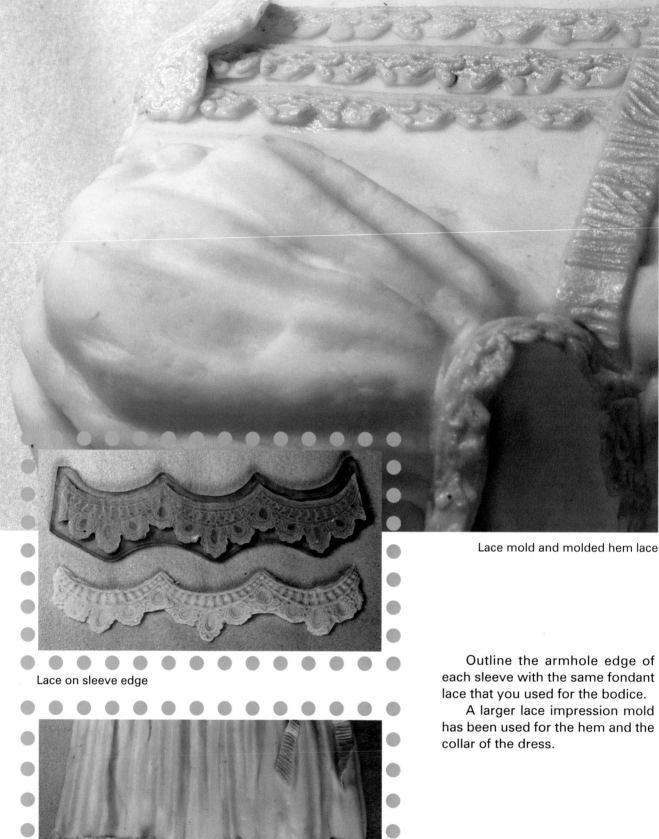

Lace mold and molded hem lace

Lace on sleeve edge

Outline the armhole edge of each sleeve with the same fondant lace that you used for the bodice.

A larger lace impression mold has been used for the hem and the collar of the dress.

Lace on hem of dress

Ribbon on dress

To form the bow on the front of the dress, use a 1/4-inch x 4-inch strip of light green fondant. Fold the right end of the strip to the center and secure it with a touch of dampness. Roll a small piece of paper towel and insert it into the loop to hold its open shape during the drying process. Repeat the process with the left end of the bow. Wrap a small piece of fondant ribbon around the center connection to resemble a knot in the bow. Mix one half teaspoon of pearl luster with two teaspoons alcoholic liquid or pure lemon extract and brush the mixture on the lace and ribbon trims to achieve a shiny appearance. When liquefying luster dust to paint with, always use a liquid with a high alcohol content. The alcohol will quickly evaporate so the piece will dry faster. If you use water, the drying process will be much longer and cause the piece to be sticky.

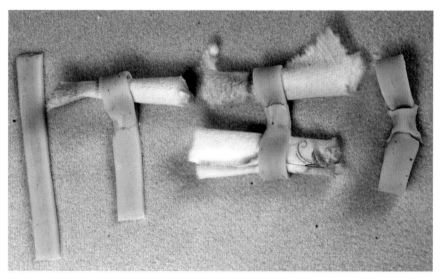

Steps to form bow

Boy's Romper

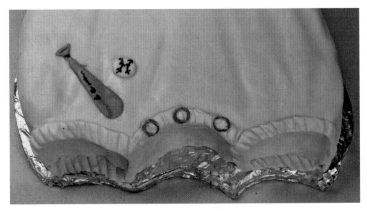

Trim on boy's romper

Carve the romper using the included pattern and crumb coat and cover with light green rolled buttercream as described for the previous "Baby Dress" cake. Because this is for a baby boy, the decorative trim is not as elaborate and has more of a masculine theme. Lightly push indentations for the leg holes to give them a 3D appearance when shaping the rolled buttercream.

Roll a thin strip of fondant and cut a 1/4- inch strip with a pizza or ribbon cutter. Slightly dampen the edges of the legs, sleeves and neck area then place the fondant strip so that it adheres to the dampened areas. Use a small rounded object such as the handle of a small paint brush or a skewer to make slight impression marks in the trim to add a pattern. Measure the distance from the shoulder to the waist of the romper and cut six 1/4-inch strips of fondant to apply to either side of the front of the romper in a vertical position. Each of these little strips should overlap the previous strip to represent tucks in the fabric. Press and smooth some fullness into the area of the romper which is at the bottom of the tucks with the warmth of your forefinger.

Tucks on boy's romper bodice

The area between the legs has the appearance of being fastened. To achieve this look, cut three grippers using the large opening of a standard decorator tip. Cut and remove a circle within the gripper with a #12 decorator tip and remove the center you cut out. Place the three grippers on the trim of the romper with a touch of moisture and brush each with silver luster and a tiny brush.

Most fathers want their little boys to be affiliated with some type of sports ball so a miniature baseball and bat seems appropriate. Tint a small amount of gum paste light brown. Roll a thin piece of brown fondant to approximately 3 inches long x 1/2 inch wide. Use the large opening of a standard decorator tip to round the tip of the bat and to cut areas at the top of the bat where it is thin. Cut the ball with the same decorator tip. Use the tip to press impressions into either side of the ball where the stitching will be placed. Add the details to the balls and bats and place them strategically on the romper.

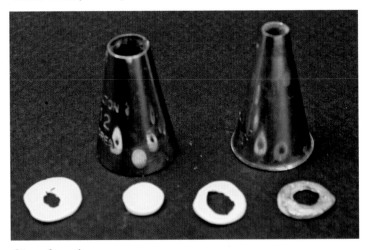

Steps for grippers

Chapter 2

Toddler to Pre-Teen

Angelic Toddler

As babies grow into toddlers and beyond, so do the celebrations that acknowledge their little lives. The angelic innocence of this curly headed toddler will delight the hearts of both young and old.

Supplies
- 2 cake layers, 8-inch x 2-inch
- 2 Tootsie Pops
- 1 pound fondant
- 2 teaspoons tylose powder
- Small rolling pin
- Toothpicks or small wooden skewers
- Food colors: brown, white, blue, pink, green
- Tiny paint brush
- Manicure scissors
- 1/2 cup royal frosting
- Large decorator tip to use as cutter
- Pink buttercream frosting
- Small heart shape cookie cutter
- Approximately one teaspoon eatable glitter
- Approximately one teaspoon piping gel

You can use gum paste or fondant to form your figures. I normally use fondant, adding two teaspoons of tylose powder to strengthen it. Mix the tylose into the paste and allow it to cure overnight in a zip lock bag before you use it.

Color a large ball of paste with a touch of pink or the appropriate color for your racial preference until you get the desired flesh color. Separate the large ball into four balls. One ball should be the same size as the Tootsie Pop and three additional balls should be twice the size of the Tootsie Pop. Keep the balls covered in a plastic bag or with plastic wrap to prevent them from drying.

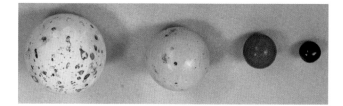

Size of balls to form baby

To form the torso, roll one larger ball until it is perfectly smooth. Hold the ball in the palm of your hand and press a Tootsie Pop into the paste until you can feel it firmly against your palm. Work the paste up over the ball. Continue to work the paste upward over the sucker stick into a pear shaped torso and smooth the body with your fingertips. Cut the exposed sucker stick 1/4-inch above the torso to aid in supporting the head later. Push a small ball tool or the end of a small rounded paintbrush into the tummy area and slightly pull down to form the navel. On the back of the baby use a small skewer or paintbrush handle to press and form a crease to mark the two sides of the little baby bottom.

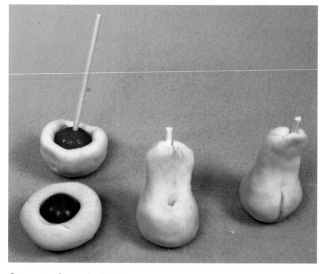

Steps to form baby torso

To form the head, roll the second large ball of paste until smooth. Repeat the process that you used to incorporate a Tootsie Pop into the torso. Cover the ball, working the excess paste to the neck where it can be trimmed. Flatten the area of the head where the eyes will be; this flattening will help to form a bulge for the puffy cheeks. Roll a tiny ball and secure for the nose. Shape the mouth exactly the same as you did for the navel by inserting a rounded object and slightly pull down and out. If you use a pacifier as in the baby picture, you will not need to form the mouth, but you will need to add the pacifier with a touch of frosting.

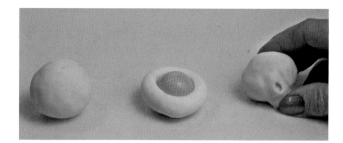

Steps to form baby head

Divide the third large ball into two equal parts to form equally sized legs. Cover one half to prevent it from drying and roll a very smooth ball with the other half. Roll the ball into a log shape. Visually divide the log in half lengthways and score lightly with the dull side of a table knife. This mark will later be the back of the knee.

Visually divide the lower half of the log shape in half again and mark for the ankle. Thin this mark between your thumb and forefinger to form the ankle.

Flatten the foot area and shape. Form the heel, cut the toes and bend the knee. Flatten the hip area to attach the leg to the body with royal frosting. Repeat this process for the other leg, being careful to make a right and a left foot. You will need to decide at this point how you will position your legs on the finished figurine and prop them to dry in that position.

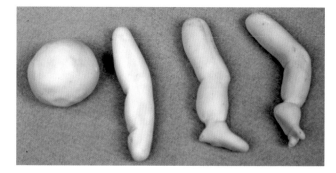

Steps to form baby legs

The arms are formed by dividing the small ball of fondant into two halves. Repeat the process described for the legs. Thin the wrist and flatten the hand. Cut a "V" shape from the hand to form the thumb. Cut the fingers with small manicure scissors and roll the fingers slightly to thin and curve them to shape. Flatten the shoulder area of the arm so it will fit. Repeat the process for the second arm, being careful to have a right and a left hand. Prop in the correct position to dry on tissues.

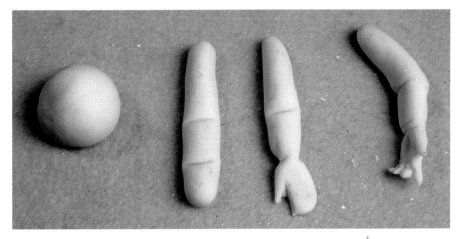

Steps to form baby arms

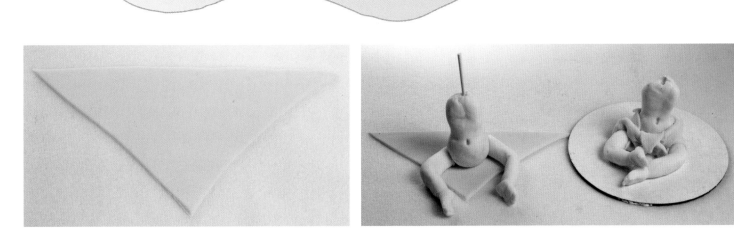

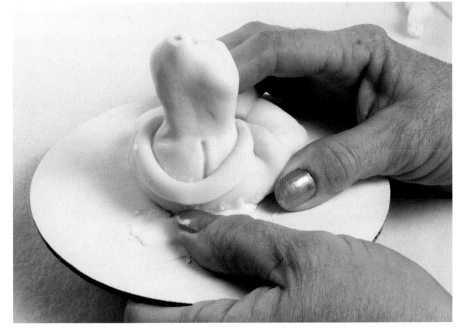

Baby diaper shape

Set baby torso on diaper

Cut a large triangle of light green fondant for the diaper. Set the baby on top of the diaper. Pull the front point of the triangle up between the baby legs. Twist the sides and bring them to the front over the top of the front point. Trim the sides if necessary and fold the front point over the twisted sides. Allow the back of the diaper to droop to show the crack in the baby bottom. Position the baby on a cake board.

Back view of diaper on baby

The features and make-up that you add to the baby will give it the angelic quality for this birthday cake. If you feel that you need practice, you can experiment on a scrap piece of fondant or even paint on waxed paper. Paint the eye area with bright white food color. Paint the iris with either blue or brown food color when the white is dry. After these two steps have dried, add a black pupil to each eye. Outline the upper half of the eye and add two or three eye lashes with a very tiny brush and black food color.

Painting face features

For the baby's pacifier, use the large end of a standard decorator tip to cut a circle from thinly rolled pink fondant. Cut a smaller circle from green paste and cut a hole from the center to form a ring. When the small circle is dry enough to hold its shape, attach it to the pink circle with a touch of royal frosting. This is the handle for the pacifier. Use a drop of royal and attach the pacifier over the mouth of the baby.

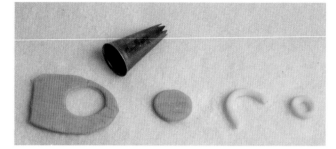

Steps for pacifier

To assemble the figurine, attach the head, securing it with royal frosting and allowing it to dry. The arms can also be attached with royal but it is necessary to prop them into position until the drying process is complete. If the figurine is for display only, it is speedier to use a glue gun

Attaching baby head to torso

Steps to form baby bib

A bib is used as baby clothing, but, in addition, it hides the connection of the head and body. Roll a thin piece of light green fondant and cut a large circle with the large opening of a cake icer tip. Use a smaller cutter to cut a half circle to form the neck opening of the bib.

The edge of the bib can be ruffled and a small appliqué such as a tiny heart or bear placed on it to add interest. Roll a thin strip of green about five inches long to form the back fastener or bow of the bib. Form and pinch together two loops and let the tails extend down the back of the baby. Attach at the back of the bib.

Placing bib on baby

Form scull cap for hair

Steps to form baby curls

The hair is formed with light brown fondant. Lay a gum ball size piece of brown in the palm of your hand and push a gum ball into it to form a cup shape. Remove the gum ball and place the cup over the head of the baby. Secure the hair with a small amount of royal frosting. Form hair lines with a modeling tool or the dull side of a table knife. Press the tool into the soft paste and pull down to blend the hair onto the neck and face.

The curls are formed by rolling tiny pieces of brown fondant around a toothpick. Remove the curls from the toothpick before they are completely dry. Slightly dampen the top of the curl and press into the soft scull cap. Start at the lower part of the back of the head and work upward in rows of curls.

I use gum balls and suckers to form the babies for several reasons. First the balls take up a lot of space and they are less expensive than gum paste or fondant. Second, this is a good way to achieve consistency in the size. Third, large pieces of gum paste often explode and using the gum ball prevents this from happening.

Close up of curls

Steps to form hearts

Stack and frost the two cake layers in pink buttercream. Place the frosted cake on a cake plate and pipe a pink ball border with tip number 10. Roll a thin piece of white fondant and cut 15-20 hearts with a small heart shaped cookie cutter. Brush each heart lightly with piping gel and dip one side of the heart into eatable glitter. Randomly place the hearts onto the pink cake.

Place the angelic toddler and a number one birthday candle on top of the cake. Sprinkle the remaining eatable glitter over the cake to complete the treat. Every little girl loves pink as well as glitz so this creation is sure to delight your toddler.

Decorated cake

Clowning Around

The angelic innocence of a toddler soon turns into the inquisitive pre-school child who begins to celebrate his independence by "clowning around."

Supplies
- 2 cake layers, 8-inch x 2-inch
- 1/2 pound white fondant, small balls of black, red, blue and green
- 2 gum balls
- 8 small gum balls
- Small rolling pin
- Pizza cutter
- Ameri-Colors white, black, red and orange
- Decorator tips # 2 and #12
- 1 cup royal frosting
- Decorator bag
- Tiny paint brush
- Small scissors

A major difference between the clown and the baby is that the baby is completely modeled in flesh tones, then dressed with appropriate clothing. The clown is molded using the color of the clown suit. In this instance, the suit is white. Experiment with various sizes of gum balls and suckers to find the correct size for your particular project. The little clown is constructed similarly to the Angelic Toddler by using gum balls rather than Tootsie Pops, which makes a slightly smaller figurine.

Various size gum balls

Make three balls of white fondant twice the size of the gum ball and one the same size. The fourth large ball is formed of flesh color for the head. Using one large white ball of fondant and any color gum ball, push the gum ball firmly into the fondant until you can feel the pressure of the ball in the palm of your hand. Work the excess paste up over the ball into a pear shaped torso.

Steps to form clown torso

Insert the second gum ball into the large flesh colored ball of fondant for the head. Push the gum ball firmly as described for forming the torso. Work the excess paste to the neck and trim it to form a very short neck. Flatten the upper half of the face where the eyes will be painted. Insert a small ball tool into the face for the mouth. Pull it down slightly and pull out. Insert a short length of spaghetti into the neck for added support when the head is placed on the torso. Set the head aside to dry.

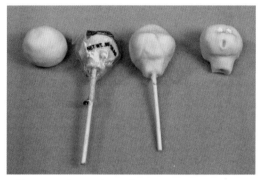

Steps to form clown face

Split the second large ball of white fondant in half so that the two legs will be equal size. Roll one half into a smooth ball. Roll the ball into a log that is approximately the length across four fingers. Find the center of the log and mark the back of the knee with the dull side of a table knife. Flatten the bottom edge of the log to form a flat place where you will attach the shoe. Bend the knee slightly, flatten the area where the leg attaches to the torso and set the pieces aside to dry.

Steps to form clown legs

The smaller white ball of fondant should be divided into half to form the arms. Form them exactly the same as described for the legs. They have the same basic shape, only smaller. Flatten the lower edge of the sleeve where the hand will attach, bend the elbow, flatten the shoulder and set aside to dry.

Roll a marble size ball of blue fondant until it is smooth. Mold

Steps to form clown arms

Steps to form shoes

the ball into a flat, oval shoe shape. It should be narrow in the center or arch area and wider at the toe. Clown shoes can be oversized and brightly colored. Press across the sole to mark the heel and around the bottom edge to mark the sole of the shoe. Repeat the process for the second shoe.

Steps to form hands

Using a small marble-size ball of flesh or pink colored fondant, roll a smooth ball. Flatten the ball into an oval pancake shape. Use pointed manicure scissors to cut a wedge shape piece from the hand which will form the thumb. Make four additional cuts for the fingers. Slightly roll each finger to smooth and shape. Place a small piece of spaghetti into the top of the hand at the wrist to aid in attaching the hand to the sleeve/arm. Repeat the procedure for the second hand, being careful to shape a right and a left hand. Set aside to dry.

Clown hat

Roll a gum ball-size piece of white fondant until it is smooth. Shape it into a cone shape. It should be pointed at the top and flat on the bottom. Bend the pointed edge slightly and attach a small green fondant ball using a short piece of spaghetti. This little ball represents a pom-pom on top of the hat. Mold the flat area on the clown's head to match the contour of the head where the hat will attach.

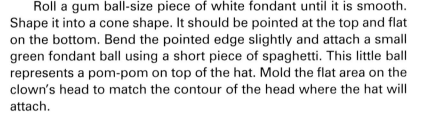
Steps for make polka dots

Roll out small, thin pieces of red, blue, and green fondant. Use the large open end of a standard decorator tip as a cutter to form bright polka dots for the clown suit. The small end of a number 12 decorator tip cuts the smaller dots. Brush the back side of each dot with gum glue or a liquid with high alcoholic content to dampen the fondant so that it will adhere to the clown suit. Position the dots randomly on the suit, arms, legs and hat.

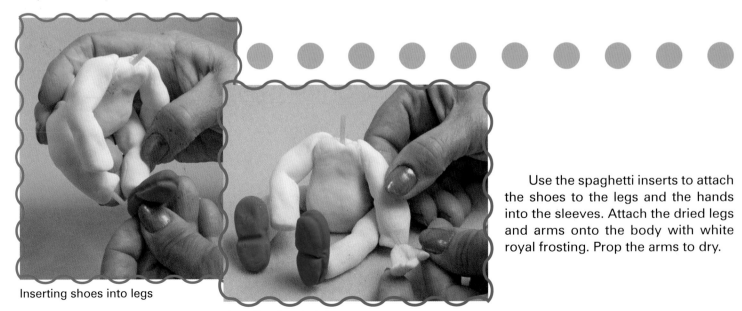
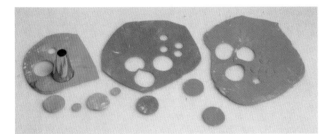
Inserting shoes into legs

Inserting hands into arms

Use the spaghetti inserts to attach the shoes to the legs and the hands into the sleeves. Attach the dried legs and arms onto the body with white royal frosting. Prop the arms to dry.

Paint large white ovals on the flat part of the face for the eyes using white food color. Allow the white to dry before painting the light blue iris and the black pupils. Paint inside the mouth with red food color. The nose is a pea-size ball of red fondant attached in place with a touch of royal frosting. Highlight the mouth and eyes with black food color and a very tiny paintbrush.

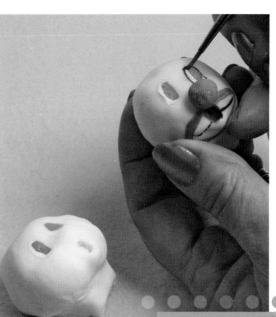

Face make up

Attach the dried head to the body with royal frosting, using the spaghetti inserts for additional support. As with the Angelic Toddler, if the clown is not to be consumed for food, the pieces will dry faster if a glue gun is used.

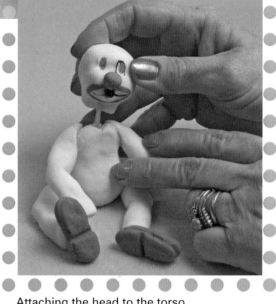

Attaching the head to the torso

Use orange royal frosting and a number 2 decorator tip to pipe hair onto the clown head. Use a circular motion to create the illusion of curly hair. Place the pointed hat onto the freshly frosted hair and pipe additional hair around the edge.

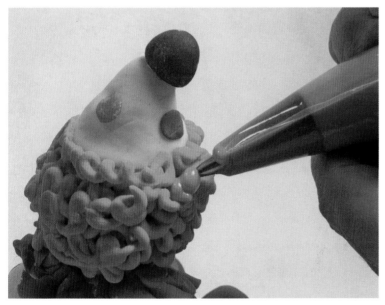

Hair for the clown

Roll a long, thin strip of red fondant and use a pizza cutter to cut 1/2-inch wide strips. Pleat the strip to form a ruffle and use the ruffles to trim the neck, sleeves and ankles of the clown.

Steps for ruffles

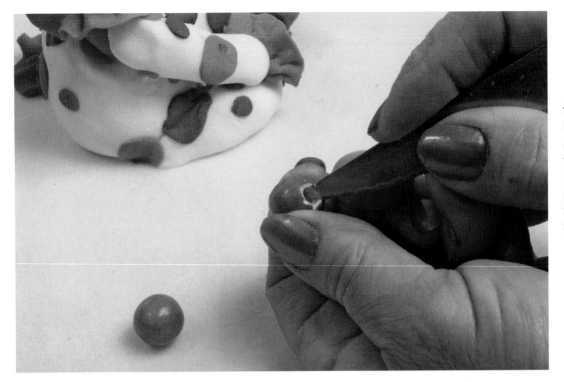

Three small gum balls form the pom-pom buttons. Use a sharp pointed knife or other sharp object to form a tiny hole in each gum ball. Insert a small piece of spaghetti in each and insert the three balls into the front of the clown suit.

Gum ball borders

Birthday candle holders

Bake two layers of cake, each 10"x 2". Cool and stack the layers using buttercream between the layers. Frost the entire cake with blue buttercream and smooth it with the paper towel method. Place brightly colored gum balls around the base of the cake to form a border, alternating colors. Glue a brightly colored ribbon around the edge of the cake board to match the color theme.

The five remaining small gum balls are used to hold the birthday candles. Make a hole in each of the balls with a sharp pointed knife that is large enough to allow the candles to be inserted. Press the holders in the soft frosting and position near the top edge of one side of the cake. Set the clown on the other side of the top so he can observe the candles. Writing the name of the child on the top front of the cake is optional. The birthday guests will experience an added treat when the gum ball borders are remove and distributed.

Brontosaurus

As children enter the pre-teenage years, their interests often turn to history, sports and even science. Although this age child has a wide scope of activities, every young boy is sure to admire a dinosaur cake to celebrate his special birthday.

Supplies
- Two 7-inch x 2-inch oval cake layers
- One 7-inch wide oval plywood cake board
- Four 1-inch diameter x 2-inch long dowels
- 4 paneling nails
- Hammer
- 6-inch x 14-inch piece of foam core board
- 1 stick pretzel
- 1 Wilton plastic hidden column
- 4 ounces white chocolate
- 12-inch x 8-inch piece of aluminum foil
- Food color in avocado and chocolate brown
- 2 pounds white buttercream
- 4 pounds of rolled fondant or rolled buttercream blended green/brown

Wooden frames are often used to enhance a special sculpted cake and to give the finished product a three dimensional appearance. Steps to create a frame are very simple and take only minimal skill with a jig saw. If you are uncomfort-

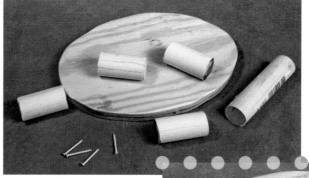

Wooden pieces for frame

able with power tools you can ask your husband or a local handyman for some assistance. Cut four 2-inch long x 1-inch diameter pieces from a 1-inch diameter x 36-inch long dowel rod. Cut an oval from thin plywood that is exactly the same size as the bottom of the 7-inch oval cake pan. The plywood should be at least 1/4-inch thick and not over one 1/2-inch. Use the dinosaur pattern included in the pattern section to position the four 2-inch long dowels under the oval plywood. Drive a paneling nail through the plywood into the dowel. These four short dowels will later become the legs for the dinosaur.

Frame assembly

Foam core board is heavier than a regular cake board. It comes in 20-inch x 30-inch sheets and is sold in most stores that sell poster board. Trace around the bottom of the 7-inch oval cake pan. Angle the tail from the rear of the oval and extend the tail an additional 7 inches to form a pointed tail. Bend the foam board so that the tail support bends downward. Cut out the shape and place it on top of the wooden frame. Secure the foam core board with frosting.

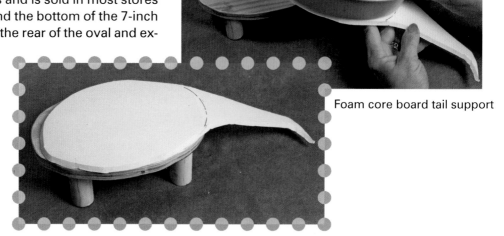

Foam core board tail support

Foam core board on stand

The neck is the most challenging part of this brontosaurus. The extended neck is formed from a large pretzel stick and white chocolate. Fold an 8-inch x 12-inch strip of aluminum foil until it is approximately 2 inches wide. Crimp the foil until it cups up into a trough or gutter shape. Pinch the foil at the top to form a round ball shape for the head. Measure 10 inches from the top of the head and bend the foil up so the chocolate will not run out. Melt four ounces of white chocolate over hot water and pour the chocolate into the aluminum foil mold. Insert the pretzel in the lower part of the mold and cover it with additional chocolate. The pretzel is not long enough for the 10-inch neck but it will give additional support to the neck where it is inserted into the hidden pillar inside the cake. Place the molded neck in the refrigerator until it is firmly set. Remove from the refrigerator and discard the foil container.

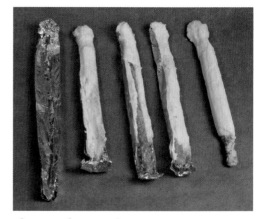

Steps to form neck

Bake and cool two 7-inch x 2-inch oval cake layers. Place the cake on the foam board and fill between the layers with buttercream. Stand a copy of the dinosaur pattern behind the cake. Use a long serrated knife to trim the cake to the contour of the pattern. Place the excess cake to the side and cut a tapered piece from this discarded cake that will fit the tail. Spread frosting on the foam core board to attach the tail pieces.

Pattern placed against cake and trimming cake

Using excess cake to form tail

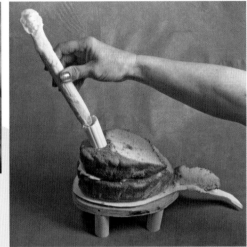

Trim hidden pillar at an angle

Inserting column into the cake

Inserted neck into support

Good support in your cake is always essential. The heavy neck of the brontosaurus is no exception. Trim one end of a Wilton hidden pillar to an angle so that it will fit securely on the bottom cake board when it is inserted into the cake at an angle.

Insert the white chocolate neck firmly into the hidden pillar support.

Crumb coat the entire cake including the legs, tail, neck and head with buttercream that is thin enough to spread easily over the cut edges.

Crumb-coated cake

Mix a batch of rolled buttercream and color it with avocado food color. Divide the frosting in two pieces. To one half add several drops of chocolate brown food color. Mix the two colors of rolled buttercream together and mix only enough to marbleize the colors. Roll out the frosting on a 12-inch x 18-inch plastic place mat or between two sheets of clear, heavy upholstery plastic. Invert the place mat so that the frosting is against the cake. Slowly peel off the plastic and press the frosting to the contour of the cake as you remove the plastic. Be gentle with the neck to prevent breakage. Trim off the excess frosting and rub the body to get the desired effect. Pinch up the back bone between your thumb and forefinger. Add extra frosting for the legs and hip area and blend them into the body with the warmth of your hands.

Use a dull table knife to form creases to the entire dinosaur covering.

Add tiny black fondant balls for eyes. Insert a thin log of white fondant into the mouth and mark creases for the teeth. For a special celebration party, carry out the theme by arranging toy dinosaurs on the table as party favors for each guest.

Close-up of forming creases/wrinkles

Chapter 3
Teen Celebrations

Makeup

The teenage years are difficult for both the teens and parents but they are full of happy years and celebratory occasions including birthdays, slumber parties, school events, proms and graduation. Being allowed to wear makeup is a milestone for young girls so fingernails, manicure tools and polish provide the theme for the first cake in the teen chapter. For those who feel uncomfortable with extensive tube decoration, this cake is probably the easiest project in the book. It is incredibly simple to construct and sure to delight any young girl.

Supplies
- 2 boxes Fruit Rollups®
- Two 8-inch x 2-inch layer cakes
- One 12-inch cake board
- 1/2 pound red chocolate coating
- 1/2 pound white chocolate coating
- 1/8 pound milk chocolate
- Pink buttercream or 1/2 pound fondant
- 1 nail equipment candy mold (CK Products)
- Paint brush
- Dusting powders, silver, pearl and pink

Bake, cool and stack the two 8-inch layers with pink frosting. Frost a 2-inch circle around the edge of the cake board with the same pink. Place the stacked cake in the center of the prepared cake board.

Starting at the top edge of the cake, place the first rollup around the cake, pushing it into the fresh frosting. Butt the second strip against the first and complete the first row. Repeat this process until the sides of the cake are completely covered with rows of the stripped rollups. The bright stripes are very inviting to a teen. Trim an additional rollup to the width of the cake board edge. Frost the edge of the board and secure the rollup around the edge.

Covering cake with fruit streamers

Place the red, white, brown/white, and red/white chocolates in small containers. To form the pink, place several pieces of white and a few red chocolate coating together. The white and chocolate can be blended to get a light tan. I have found that it is very easy to heat water in an electric skillet then set small cups of chocolate into the warm water. The thermostat can be set to maintain a regulated temperature that is not too hot. Do not get the water too deep because a drop of water will cause the chocolate to thicken and seize up.

Preparing chocolate to melt

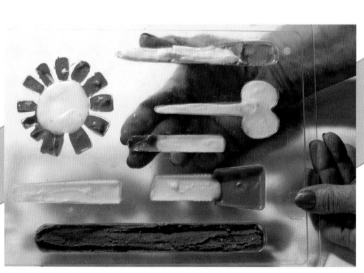

Molding chocolate in fingernail candy mold

Fill the candy mold with the appropriate color chocolate. If you want two colors such as the nail polish bottle, first put white into the mold to represent the lid and place the mold in the refrigerator until it sets. Remove the mold from the refrigerator and fill the polish bottle with red. Place the mold in the refrigerator again until it is chilled.

Remove chocolate from mold

Remove the mold from the refrigerator. Invert the mold and lightly tap so that the chocolate items fall out. If you have difficulty removing the chocolate it probably is not cold enough. Repeat the procedure for all of the makeup items.

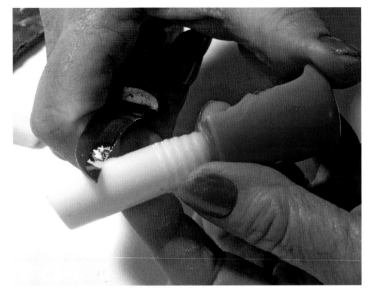

Trimming edges with small knife

Use a sharp knife to trim all excess chocolate from the individual pieces. The trimmings can be placed in the appropriate color chocolate and re-melted.

Highlighting with pearl luster

To highlight the items you can brush pearl luster onto the white items, such as the polish lid and the base of the lip stick.

Brushing clippers with silver luster

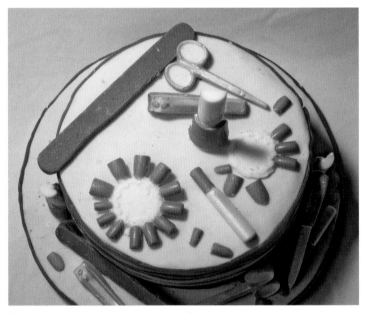

Arrange nail equipment on top of cake

The nail clippers, scissors and file are brushed with silver dusting powder. The handle of the file is brushed with pink dusting powder.

Arrange the items randomly on the top and sides of the cake. Secure the pieces with small amounts of frosting to prevent them from slipping off when the cake is moved.

First Car

The highlight of being a teenager is the birthday when they are eligible for a driver's license, which in turn leads to the responsibility and freedom of their first car. This snappy red convertible is the perfect way to celebrate.

Supplies
- Car pan, Wilton Industries
- 2 cake batters baked in car pan
- 1 sheet of 1/4-inch foam core board
- Glue gun
- One 12-inch x 18-inch cake board
- Several pieces heavy spaghetti
- Black and white buttercream
- One 18-inch x 14-inch piece of clear upholstery plastic
- Rolling pin
- One clear gelatin sheet which can be ordered from Conway's Confections
- 4 round sugar cookies
- Spatula
- 1/4 pound black fondant
- 1/8 pound white fondant and red fondant
- Serrated knife
- Decorator tips #789, 104, 124
- 3 pounds red rolled buttercream

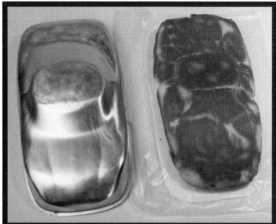

Car pan and baked cake

Bake, cool and invert the car cake. This pan is designed to sit directly on the cake board. Although I personally like the 3 dimensional appearances that a frame gives to the car, you have the option of eliminating the frame.

Using a serrated or sharp knife, cut around the roof area of the car top. Remove this cake piece and trim out the interior until the cake is approximately 1/2-inch thick on the car floor. Try to cut the back area at an angle so the seats will lean backward. Frost the interior with black buttercream.

Cutting out interior area

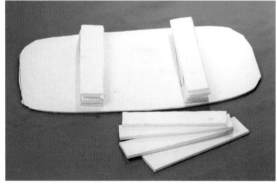

Frame for car

Trace around the base of the car cake pan on a sheet of foam core board. Use a sharp knife to cut the board approximately 1/4-inch smaller than the marked line. Cut eight 1-1/2-inch wide x 6-1/2-inch strips. Glue 4 of these strips together to form a car axle. Repeat for the rear axle. You can use any type of glue, but hot glue is fast and works as long as it does not make contact with the cake or any eatable parts. Mark the position where you want the wheels and glue the two axles in place. Glue the bottom of both axle strips, invert the frame and glue into position on the base cake board.

Place the car cake on the completed frame and completely frost with white buttercream. Fill in any gaps or cracks between the cake and the frame.

Crumb-coated car on frame

Roll two balls of black fondant, each approximately the size of a golf ball. Roll one of the balls and elongate into a fat oval. Slightly bend the oval into a right angle. Use your thumb to firmly press a seat into the lower position of the oval. Reverse ends and firmly press your thumb into the black oval to form the seat back. Repeat for the second bucket seat. Position the seats into the interior of the car, leaning both toward the back of the car.

Forming bucket seats

Forming steering wheel

Roll out a small ball of black fondant to form the steering wheel. Use the large opening of icer tip #789 to cut a circle. Make openings in the wheel with a tip #104.

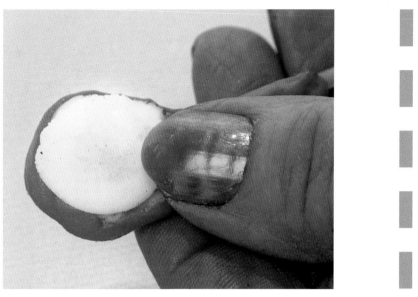

Side mirrors

Form the mirrors and lay aside. Break two small pieces of spaghetti. Push one end of the spaghetti into a ball of red fondant. Smooth the ball area and flatten it into a small flat pancake shape. Work the excess half way down the spaghetti to insert into the side of the car. Cut a small round white circle with the open end of a decorator tip. Dampen the white circle and place on the front side of the mirror. Repeat the procedure for the second mirror.

Steps for gear shift

To form the stick shift place a pea size ball of white fondant onto the end of a 2-inch piece of spaghetti. Smooth the small ball and work the excess down the shaft of the spaghetti. Paint the knob and shifter with silver luster and lay aside to dry.

Steps to form hubcaps

Lay 4 round sugar cookies on a piece of waxed paper and frost the front and edges of each with black buttercream frosting. Allow the wheels to dry. To form the hub caps, roll out a small piece of white fondant. Use the open end of a large decorator tip to cut 4 circles. With the 104 tip, cut 6 sections from each circle to form the spoke areas. When the hub caps are dry you can paint them with a mixture of a 1/2 teaspoon of silver luster powder with 1/2 teaspoon vodka to liquefy it. Paint the hubcaps and allow them to dry before placing them on the wheels. Secure the hub caps to the wheels with a small amount of frosting.

Rolling out rolled buttercream

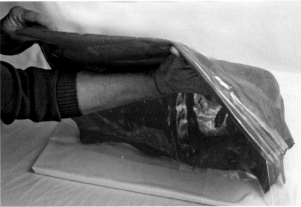

Lift with plastic intact

Flatten the piece of clear upholstery plastic and rub it with a small amount of powdered sugar. Roll out a large piece of the red rolled buttercream until it covers the 14-inch x 18-inch piece of plastic. Trim the edges. Carefully lift the plastic and invert it over the crumb-coated cake. With the plastic intact, rub the sides, front, and rear of the car to adhere it to the cake. Starting at one side, gently remove the plastic from the frosting and continue to smooth.

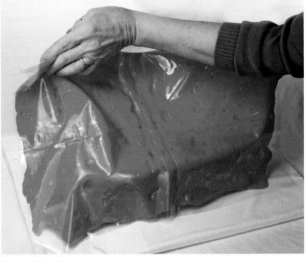

Drape frosting over car

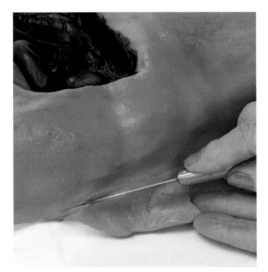

Trimming excess frosting

Molding fenders over wheels

The area of frosting laying over the interior will droop down. Do not rub this area. Use scissors to cut out this piece of frosting to expose the black interior. Rub the areas around the interior to adhere them to the car. Trim the excess frosting around the frame with a small knife and discard. Cut half circle areas over the axles where the tires are to be attached. Use frosting to secure the wheels over the axles. With your thumb and forefinger gently mold the fondant into a ridge around the tire to represent the fender area. Use the same process to mold the front and rear bumpers.

Break a piece of spaghetti approximately 6 inches long. Brush 3 inches of the antenna with silver luster. Do not paint the area that will be inserted into the cake.

Painting silver antenna

Steps for convertible top

To form the convertible top roll a piece of red fondant approximately 4 inches x 8 inches. Lift the piece of fondant and gently lay over three 8-inch pieces of dowel or PVC pipe. Rub the fondant to the contour of the pipes so that you have 3 ridges and 3 groves. Pinch each end of the 3 ridges together. Bend approximately two inches at each end of the piece to form right angles. Trim off any excess and fit to the rear of the car so it resembles the convertible top in a lowered position. Secure in place with frosting.

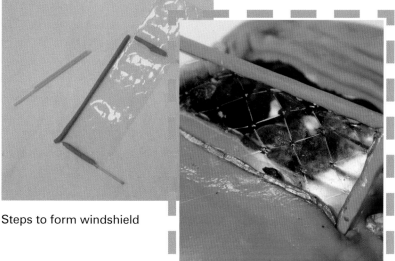

Steps to form windshield

Close-up of windshield

To form the windshield frame break three pieces of the heavy spaghetti. The two side support pieces are each 3 inches long and the one piece for the top of the frame is 4 inches long. Cover 1-1/2-inch of each side piece with red fondant. Leave the area that is to be inserted into the cake without covering. Cover the 4-inch top piece. Cut a piece of the gelatin sheet to fit the approximately 1-1/2-inch x 4-inch frame. Stick the side pieces into the cake. Lay the top support on top of the two side pieces. Use a small amount of frosting around the edge of the gelatin windshield and press the sheet onto the back side of the frame to secure it.

To finish the interior of the car place the gear shift between the bucket seats, the steering wheel on the dash and two white circles for the instrument panel. Add the antenna and side mirrors. The head lights and tail lights are cut out and white pieces of fondant are inserted. Outline the lights, grill and hood ornament with silver luster that has been liquefied. Cut a 1-inch x 2-inch piece of white fondant and add for the license plate. Use a food safe marker to add a significant name or number.

Interior of car

Graduation

As the teen years near an end they are usually climaxed by a high school graduation. This will probably be the last big celebration you will share with your child before they leave for college so you need to create something special. This whimsical little brainy owl will symbolize your child's intelligence and show your pride in their accomplishments.

Supplies
- One 8-inch square by 2-inch tall cake
- One 12-inch square cake board
- 2 cup shaped ice cream cones
- 1 Tootsie pop
- 1 graham cracker
- # 4,12, and 102 decorator tips
- Royal frosting in white, tan, dark brown and green
- Marble size balls of orange, yellow and black fondant
- White buttercream or fondant
- Green buttercream or fondant
- Clay gun
- One sheet wafer paper

Spread a little royal frosting on one ice cream cone and place it inside of the second cone. It is best to use royal because the grease from buttercream frosting will be absorbed and collapse the cones.

Secure cones with royal

Roll a ball of white fondant the size of a walnut. Lay the ball in the palm of your hand and press the Tootsie pop into the ball. Work the fondant over the sucker until it is completely covered. Trim off the excess fondant from around the sucker stick. Press the sucker stick firmly into the top of the stacked cones. Roll a piece of fondant approximately 2 inches wide x 4 inches long and wrap around the top part of the upper cone. This will form a fat stomach for the owl. Press the ends together to secure in the back and around the neck area.

Forming head and body

Use dark brown frosting and a small spatula to cover the stump area that the owl is sitting on. Use an up and down motion and leave the surface rough to resemble bark.

Place a #12 decorator tip into a bag of white royal frosting. Starting at the stump area make a row of tear drop shape feathers where the stomach area will be. Overlay with the second and third rows of white tear drop feathers until they reach the neck.

Brown stump area

Forming rows of white feathers

49

Steps for owl head

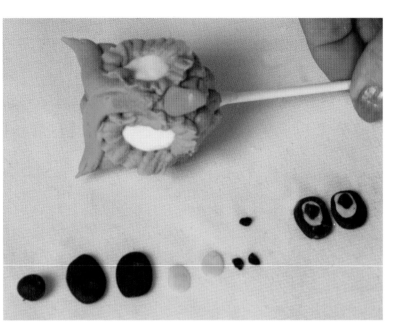

Steps for owl eyes

Make two white ovals with the royal to mark the eyes. When the frosting begins to air dry, flatten slightly. Start at the neck edge and pipe rows of tear drop shaped tan feathers onto the head. Pipe a short horn on either side. Beginning at the center front between the eyes, pipe a long eye brow area that extends over the horns. Use a #102 decorator tip and tan royal to form a ruffle around each eye.

The eyes are formed by making a series of small flat ovals. Form two black ovals topped by two smaller yellow ovals which will be completed with a very small black dot to represent the pupil of the eye. Assemble the pieces, dampen the back and place on the white of the eyes. Start the beak with a pea-size ball of orange fondant. Shape into a long, pointed beak shape. Insert a small piece of spaghetti to aid in anchoring it to the face of the owl.

Six claws are formed from pea-shape balls. Elongate each ball and curve slightly for a claw. Let dry slightly and place at the base of the owl onto the stump.

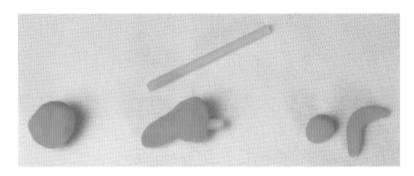

Steps for forming beak and claws

Starting at the top edge of the stump and the side of the white feathers, pipe rows of tan feathers that overlap and completely cover the body of the owl. Pipe three longer feathers to form the tail of the owl.

The wings are made with long tear drop shape lines. Start at the lower, middle side and curve a long line from the side to the neck of the owl. Above this line pipe a shorter second and third curved line. Repeat this process for the other wing.

Brown feathers and tail

Wing feathers

Steps to form graduate hat

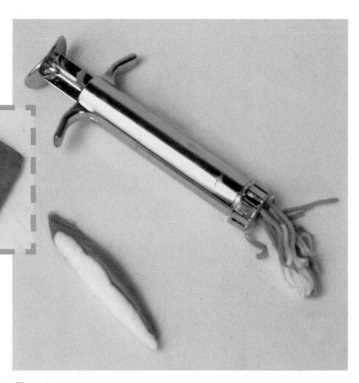

Tassels

Roll a 3-inch x 5-inch piece of green fondant. Lay the graham cracker onto one end of the fondant and cover with the other half. Seal the edges and smooth to form the hat. To form the tassels for the hat and borders, blend a small piece of green with a piece of white fondant and place inside a clay gun. Press down the plunger very hard to press the fondant through the small holes and form strings. Cut off with a sharp knife and press the top together to form a tassel. A small round, flat green dot of fondant is used to cover the connections.

Cut a piece of wafer paper that is 3-1/2 inches wide x 5 inches long. Start at one side edge and tightly roll into a cylinder. Dampen at a center point and lay something onto the connection until it dries. Place the diploma at the base of the owl and pipe a green ribbon onto the center with a decorator tip #4 and green royal frosting. Position the owl onto the upper left corner of the frosted cake and secure it with white royal frosting. Pipe #4 string work around the edge of the cake and add a tassel at each point. Complete the cake with a beading border and the appropriate congratulations message which could include the year or the name of the graduate. Because the owl figurine is made from royal it will last indefinitely if covered in an air tight container and made well in advance of the party.

Forming diploma

Chapter 4

Wedding Celebrations

• • • • • • • • •

Gift Box

Children grow up. As they leave the teen years, the cycle of life begins for a new generation and more events evolve to be celebrated with cake. Occasions to be celebrated for young adults, like engagement parties, showers, wedding cakes, bachelor parties, and groom's cakes are all featured in this chapter.

There are numerous types of showers that can be hosted for the happy couple, including personal, household, lingerie, kitchen, bath, couples, and many more, all of which could be personalized in cake.

The depiction of a gift box to blend with hues of the bridal color or theme is a very personal and popular design. The size of the cake should be determined by the size of the crowd. For a large crowd you can make numerous packages. Some can be stacked while others are randomly placed on the table.

Supplies
- 1 two-layer 8-inch square cake
- 1/2 pound fondant tinted blue
- Wilton blue delphinium paste color
- Ameri-Color Sky Blue gel color
- Wedgwood Blue Crystal dusting powder
- One 12-inch cake board
- One 3-foot length of 1/2-inch diameter PVC pipe or ribbon drying rack
- Small maple leaf cookie cutter
- Buttercream frosting
- Ribbon cutting tool or pizza cutter
- 1/2 cup blue royal frosting
- Ribbon embossing roller optional

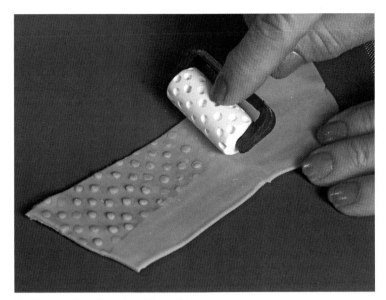

Rolling and embossing blue ribbon

Cutting ribbon with a ribbon cutter

Form the bow in advance by coloring the 1/2 pound of fondant with 1/4 teaspoon Wilton delphinium blue paste color and one drop of America Color sky blue gel color. Blend the mixture thoroughly. Divide a golf ball size ball and place the remainder in a plastic bag to prevent drying. Knead the ball until it is smooth then elongate it. Roll the oblong piece of fondant on a surface that is lightly coated with powdered sugar. Roll the fondant until it is very thin, but thick enough to hold together if you lift the sheet of fondant.

For textured designs place the design roller in center of the thin sheet of fondant and roll to each end. It is best to use the palm of your hand to apply pressure to the roller in order to achieve a clearer pattern.

Ribbon cutters can be purchased from various supply shops or you can create your own. The cutters come with various length spacers so that you can form wide or narrow strips. Place the 1-inch spacer on the cutter. Cut long strips from the pre-rolled piece of fondant. The length of the strips will determine the ribbon loop size. For the pictured bow, cut 4-inch long strips.

If you do not have access to a ribbon cutter, you can mark 1-inch strips with a ruler and cut them with a pizza cutter.

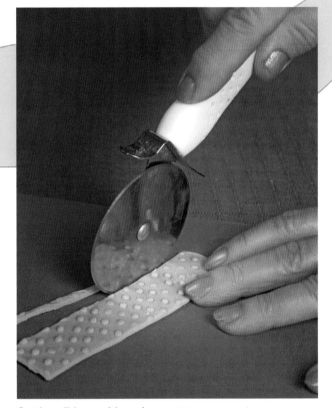

Cutting ribbon with a pizza cutter

Numerous types of drying racks can be purchased but you can easily construct one with available materials. Any length 1/2-inch PVC water pipe that has been thoroughly washed is the perfect diameter to dry ribbon loops. The ends of the pipe must be supported at a height so the loops do not touch the table. In this photo two rolls of paper towels are used as supports.

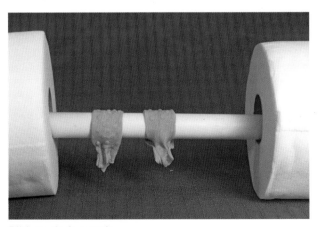

Ribbon drying rack

Lift a length of fondant from the table and place over the PVC drying rack. Slightly dampen one end of the loop and press the ends together with your fingertips to secure it around the pipe. Repeat the process until you have at least 24 loops. It is always better to make a few extra loops to allow for breakage. Check the loops occasionally to be sure that they are not sticking to the pipe. Allow the loops to dry overnight before removing them from the pipe. To remove, lift one end of the pipe and slide the loops off of the end.

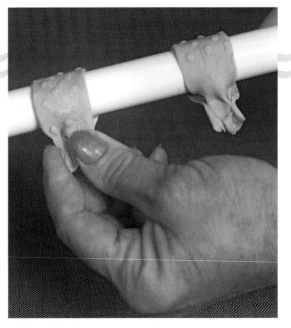

Place ribbons on rack to dry

Circle base for bow

Loops on base to start bow

Make a base for the bow by rolling a small ball of blue fondant to an 1/8-inch thickness. Cut a circle with a large jar lid or other cutter that is approximately 2-1/2 to 3 inches diameter. Place the circle on a piece of waxed paper and allow it to dry while the loops are drying.

To assemble, leave the base on the waxed paper and spread a thick coat of royal frosting over the base. Place a ring of the loops around the base edge so that the ends are secure in the royal frosting and the loops extend over the edge of the base. Place a mound of royal in the center of the ring of loops. Add a second ring of loops on top of the first ring, alternating the loops so that they are positioned between the loops of the first row. The first row of loops lays flat on the base but each additional row is elevated. Add another mound of frosting in the center and continue adding rings of loops until the bow is full and fluffy. Set the bow aside and allow it to dry before removing the waxed paper.

The loops will accumulate a powered sugar coating during the formation process. To remove this sugar and to intensify the color, brush each loop with pearl dusting powder and leave the bow to dry.

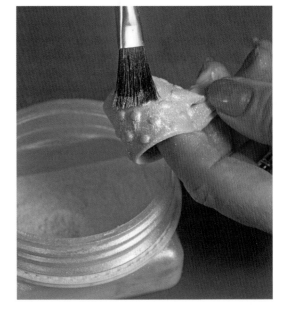

Brush loops with luster dust

Ribbon curls

Completed bow

To form long curled ribbons, roll and impress additional pieces of fondant as previously described but cut these into narrow strips — not more than 1/2-inch wide and cut into various lengths. Roll each piece tightly around a dowel rod. Lay the assembly aside to dry approximately fifteen minutes. Before the strips are totally dry and brittle, gently remove the dowel rod and drape the curls over the corners of the tiers, attaching at the bow edge. It may be necessary to place a spot of royal frosting under the curls to hold them in the position that you desire.

Cut leaves and vein

Color leaves Wedgwood blue

To form leaves, roll a small ball of white fondant until thin. Use the smallest leaf cutter of the Wilton fall leaf cookie cutters to cut numerous leaves from the white fondant. Use a dull table knife to form a center vein and a few to the sides of the leaf.

Move each leaf to a curved flower former to shape the leaves.

When the leaves are dry, brush each leaf with a medium width brush and Wedgwood blue dusting powder. Position the leaves around and between the grape clusters to form a solid border around the base of the cake. For an added enhancement, brush the grape clusters lightly with pearl luster.

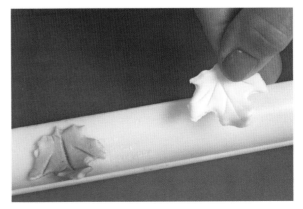

Place leaves in a flower former

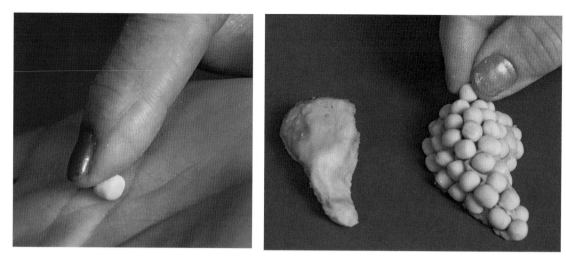

Roll and shape grapes in hand

Pipe a mound of frosting and cover with grapes

The theme for the chosen wedding cake was borrowed from the Blue Wedgwood china pattern which has various designs of white on blue and blue on white, incorporating grapes, feathers, and other patterns. Even if you are not familiar with the Wedgwood patterns, grapes have long signified a fruitful marriage. Our featured wedding cake is blue with white so the shower cake colors are reversed to highlight a white cake with blue trim. To form a border around the base of the package use blue grape clusters and leaves.

To form blue grapes, roll a small piece of blue fondant to an approximately 1/4-inch thickness and cut small circles with a #10 decorator tip. Roll each little piece in the palm of your hand until it is smooth and round.

Approximately 24 grapes are needed for each cluster. The grapes can be made in advance to save preparation time on the actual cake.

When the cake is frosted, pipe mounds of blue buttercream around the base of the box cake and cover each with the individual dried grapes and arrange with leaves to form the border for the cake.

• •

Stack and frost the cooled two layer cake. Any type frosting is suitable, but fondant is pictured for its photogenic qualities. Gift box cakes can be decorated with any variety of designs or left plain with a box lid and ribbons.

To form a box lid appearance, roll a strip of white fondant that is the length of the circumference of the box and 1-inch wide by 1/8-inch thick. Lightly dampen around the top edge of the cake and wrap the inch-wide strip of fondant around the cake, keeping the top edge of the strip even with the top edge of the cake. Keep checking the strip to assure that it does not slide down.

Roll, emboss and cut four strips of the blue ribbon that are approximately six inches long. These will form ribbons around the sides of the gift box. Place the end of one strip at the center base of one side and let it lay up and over to the center top of the cake. Repeat for the three remaining sides. Cut two shorter 1-inch strips and emboss for ribbon tails. Cut each tail three to four inches long and trim the exposed end into a "V" shape. Add each to the top of the cake and twist or prop a little to give the ribbon some movement. Add the curled ribbons and place the fluffy bow on the center top of the package.

Close-up of grape border

Side ribbon design

Something Blue

The wedding cake is second in importance only to the wedding gown, so much thought and creativity should go into the design. The pure white creation of the past has given way to colorful, whimsical, personalized, and theme cakes. The Wedgwood or fruitful theme of our selected wedding was described in the previous shower gift box cake. The leaves and grapes on the wedding cake are not pearlized but remain dull white to resemble bisque china.

Supplies
- 14-inch, 10-inch, and 6-inch two-layer tiers of cake
- 1 pound white fondant
- 1/4 pound blue fondant
- 6-8 pounds blue buttercream frosting
- Delphinium blue paste color
- Ameri-Color sky blue color
- Small leaf cookie cutter (Wilton)
- Table knife
- Flower former
- #10 decorator tip
- 1 medium size gum ball
- 1 medium size wedge brush
- 1 bolt blue ribbon for edge of board

In advance form white fondant leaves for all borders of the cake as described in directions for the Gift Box cake — cut, vein and dry. Do not color these leaves, but leave bisque white.

Making white leaves

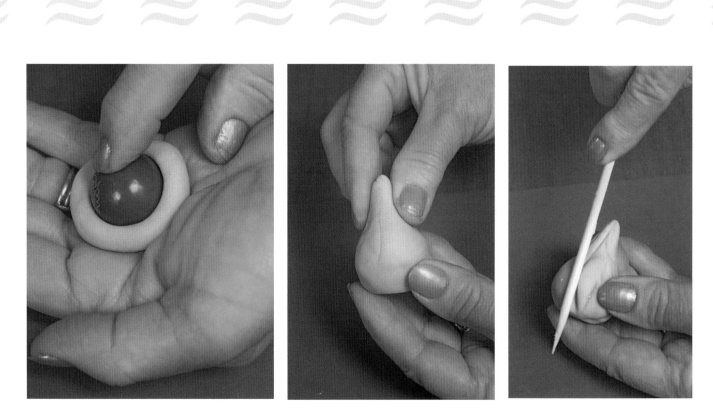

Forming ball for top – gum ball in paste   Pointed ball   Mark pointed ball with skewer

The top tier of the wedding cake resembles a keepsake box with a pointed knob or handle on top. To form the knob, roll a ball of blue fondant until it is smooth. Place it into the palm of your hand and firmly press a gum ball into the paste until it is hidden.

Smooth the ball and rub and pull it into a point.

Use a skewer or other small rounded object to press vertical lines from the top to the bottom of the knob and set aside to dry.

Frosted 10" cake

Mark area for the top layer

Types of supports

Inserting dowel in cake

Bake all layers and cool thoroughly. The layers should be as level as possible, so if the cake mounds up in the center, use a long serrated knife to trim it until it is level. Invert one layer onto a cake board that is the same size, the14-inch cake on a 14-inch board, the 10-inch cake on a 10-inch board, and the 6-inch cake on a 6-inch board. Invert the second layer of each size, placing waxed paper between the board and the cake so that it can be moved again. Frost the top of the first layer. Turn the inverted second layer onto the top of the first layer. The two cake bottoms are now together in center of the cake tier. Remove the waxed paper and frost the entire tier with buttercream. Some decorators prefer to crumb coat the cake then cover it with a heavier coat. Others only do one coat of frosting. After the final coat, allow the frosting to air dry until it is powdery feeling to the touch. Place a paper towel without a design on the cake and rub until the surface of the cake is perfectly smooth.

Proper construction of a tiered wedding cake is of utmost importance. Just like a skyscraper, if it does not have a good foundation and proper supports it will lean and possibly fall. Various instructors offer various techniques for stacking but I suggest what has been proven to work for me through many trials and errors.

To mark a placement for the supports, lay a cake board on top of the cake and mark around the board with a skewer, toothpick, or other pointed object. The board should be the size of the cake which will be stacked on top of the first. For example, if a six-inch cake will set on an eight-inch cake, you would use a 6-inch cake board to mark the position. Remove the cardboard and there will be a perfect 6-inch marked circle on top of the cake.

● ● ● ● ● ● ● ● ● ● ● ● ● ● ● ● ● ● ●

Numerous materials are available that can be used to support the weight of each additional tier. Pictured are 1/4-inch dowel rod, 1/2-inch PVC pipe, and 10-inch hidden pillar. Four of the 1/4-inch dowels are sufficient to support a small tier but the 1/2-inch PVC is more dependable for larger layers.

Push the supports straight down within the marked area on top of the cake. If it is crooked or tilted it could cause the cake to fall. After the supports are in position, set the cake straight down within the marked area over the supports. Do not slide the cake or it could cause the supports to lean and minimize the effectiveness of the supports.

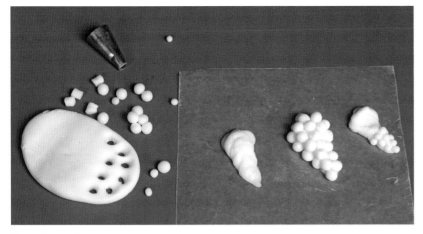

Form two sizes of grapes using the same procedure as described for the Gift Box cake. The tiny grapes for the box lid are formed with a #10 decorator tip and the fondant is 1/16-inch thick. The larger grapes for the borders of the cake use the same #10 decorator tip with the fondant 1/4-inch thick.

Two sizes of grapes

Feather steps

The feather pattern is piped directly onto the middle tier of the wedding cake. Using a #10 decorator tip and white frosting, start at the top edge of the tier and pipe a large backward "S". Use a medium wedge-shaped brush to create the feathers. Starting at the base of the design, place the brush slightly to the right of the design center and pull the excess frosting to the side, forming a thin layer of frosting that creates a part of the feather. Continue the movement until the top of the design is reached. Repeat the procedure on the left side of the feather. Start slightly to the left of the center and pull the design to the left.

Close-up of feathers

Close-up of grapes around base

Pipe mounds of white frosting randomly around the base of the cake and cover each mound with the larger size pre-formed grapes. Approximately 24 grapes are needed for each cluster. Pipe curls and stems with a #4 decorator tip and white frosting. Pre-formed white leaves are placed strategically around the base. Repeat the process around the base of all tiers.

Close-up of all borders

Close-up of box top edge

Top of box grapes and ball

To form the appearance of a box lid, cut a 1-inch wide strip of blue fondant the circumference of the top layer and place around the top edge of the top layer. Specific steps are described for the Gift Box lid. Place the pre-formed knob in the center of the top. Around the knob, pipe mounds of white frosting and cover each with the smaller size grapes to form grape clusters around the top of the box. Add leaves and curls to complete the design.

Chocolate for the Groom

Groom's cakes are very popular, especially in the south, but regardless of the location they are always fun and a good conversation topic. They can be as simple as a luscious looking chocolate and strawberries or something that represents the groom's hobbies or occupation.

Supplies
- 1 two-layer 8-inch x 2-inch round cake
- 2 quarts fresh strawberries
- 1 box mini chocolate mints
- 2 pounds chocolate buttercream
- 1 pound chocolate melted
- 1 #4 or #5 decorator tip
- 2 disposable decorator bags
- #18 star decorator tip
- One 10-inch cake plate or board
- Small piece of poster or cardboard for pattern

Pattern for the swirls　　　　　　　　　　　　　　　　Chocolate swirls

　　Make a pattern for your chocolate swirls by drawing circles on a piece of poster or cardboard. The outside ring of the circle should be 1-1/2 inches to 2 inches in diameter. A half dollar or small bottle lid can be used to form the circles. Leave enough space between the circles so that they do not touch. Cover the cardboard with clear plastic wrap. Smooth the wrap and tape on back of the cardboard to hold it in place. Place a #4 decorator tip in a disposable plastic decorator bag. Put approximately one cup of melted chocolate into the bag. Start at the center of the circle and pipe around the circle until you reach the outside edge of the pattern. Continue making circles until the patterns are covered. Place in the refrigerator to harden until ready to use.

Frosting 8" cake　　　　　　　　　　　　　　　　　Drizzle edge with chocolate

　　Assemble the cooled cake with chocolate frosting between the layers. Frost the entire cake in chocolate and smooth with a paper towel.

　　Dip melted chocolate with a tablespoon and drizzle around the outside edge of the cake top. Allow the melted chocolate to drip over the side of the cake at various lengths. It will harden as it runs down. Continue drizzling spoonfuls until you complete the top.

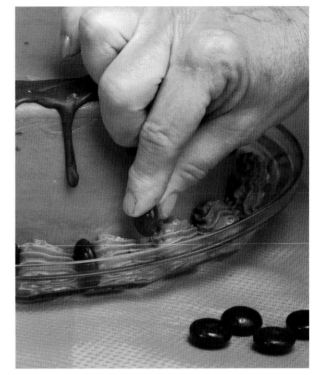

Shell border

Pipe a chocolate buttercream border around the lower edge of the cake with a #18 star tip in a disposable decorator bag to form a continuous line of shells.

Place a mini chocolate mint between each shell to add additional chocolate contrast and taste.

Adding mints to border

Arranging strawberries

Remove curls from plastic wrap

Place curls on top

Arrange the strawberries on top of the cake. Select berries that are approximately the same height. Dip the stem end in the melted chocolate and place on the edge of the top.

Carefully remove one of the chocolate curls from the plastic wrap and lightly dip in the chocolate. Place the curl against the first strawberry. Barely dip the curl into the chocolate because if it gets too warm, it will collapse.

Dip another strawberry and place against the curl. Continue this procedure until the top of the cake is covered with berries and curls. You will have a simple to make creation that looks absolutely luscious.

Close up of strawberries

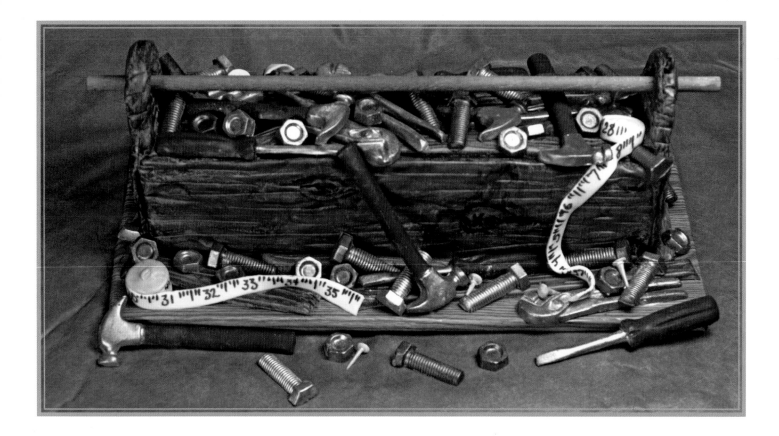

Honey Do Box

A well known fact among newly wed couples is that soon after the wedding festivities have passed, the reality of married life sets in and numerous trivial chores seem to pop up. These are known as "Honey Do" jobs because it seems the new bride is always saying, "Honey could you do this or Honey could you do that?" With this in mind the "Honey Do" fix-it box could attribute a note of humor to any of the wedding parties.

Supplies
- 1 long loaf pan cake, 4-1/2-inch x 16-inch
- Cake board, 12-inch x 19-inch
- Wood grain contact paper
- 1 dowel rod, 20 inches long x 1/2 inch diameter
- 1 tool candy mold
- 1 nuts and screws candy mold
- Chocolate frosting
- Luster dust, bronze and silver
- Dusting powder, poinsettia red
- Food writer pen
- Brown America-Color food color
- Several medium size paint brush
- 2 pounds chocolate
- Table knife
- Small sharp knife
- Small piece of foam core board for ends (locate in pattern section)
- #10 decorator tip
- 1/4 pound white fondant
- 1/2 cup white royal frosting

Tool mold filled with chocolate

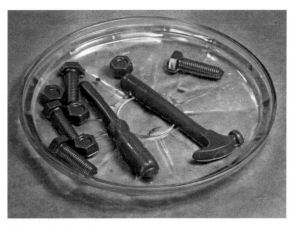

Unmolded tools

Melt chocolate in a bowl over warm water. Use a spoon to dip the melted chocolate and pour into the tool and screws candy molds. Tap gently on the table to remove air bubbles that might accumulate in the chocolate. Place the filled candy molds into the refrigerator until firmly set.

After the candy is chilled, remove the mold from the refrigerator and invert to remove the candy from the mold. Tap gently on the mold to remove. If the candy remains in the mold, it needs to chill longer.

Trim all the edges and excess chocolate with a small, sharp knife. The trimmings can be added back to the chocolate pot and re-melted.

Trimming tools

Brushing tools with color

Brushing the tools with color makes them more realistic. Any color can be used but the hammers and screwdrivers pictured have the handles brushed with poinsettia red dusting powder.

The hammer head, screwdriver and pliers are brushed with silver. Part of the screws and bolts and brushed with silver and others with copper luster for a realistic appearance. If you brush your pieces over a piece of waxed paper, you can capture the excess and use again.

Brushing screws with color

To form tape measures, cut a long 1/2-inch wide strip of white fondant. Start at one end and roll the tape. Leave several inches of the tape unrolled. Allow the tape to dry then mark numbers and inches with a food safe pen. For variety a round circle can be made for a top and bottom cover of the tape.

Forming tape measure

Numerous nails are simple to make to add interest to the tool box. Roll a small piece of white fondant approximately 1/8-inch thick. Cut numerous circles with a #10 decorator tip. Press each of these circles with your fore finger to flatten and form the head of the nail. Use a tiny ball of white fondant about the size of a small pea to form the nail which is pointed on one end. Allow the pieces to dry then assemble the head to the nail with a drop of royal frosting. Let the nails dry to secure the heads then brush with silver luster dust.

Forming nail

Pieces of boards, planks, or lumber are very simple to make and are a good filler for the box. Roll a piece of brown fondant approximately 1/4-inch thick and cut various width and length boards. The boards pictured are 1-inch wide. Use a dull table knife to imprint marks to resemble the grain in the lumber. Brush the boards with brown liquid color that has been thinned with a few drops of vodka or other fast evaporating liquid. Allow to dry before placing on the cake.

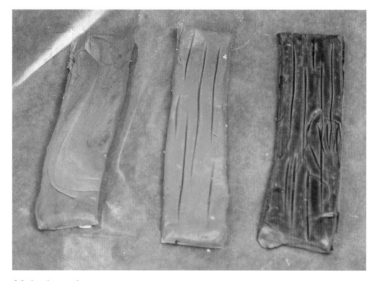

Make boards

Cover cake

Form board marks

Bake and thoroughly cool the long loaf cake. Place it on a wood grain-covered board and frost it with brown frosting (either buttercream or fondant will work). Use the table knife to form board marks on the cake. Brush additional brown liquid color over the cake. If you want additional detail you can paint darker board marks or wood designs.

Brush cake with color

Foam ends

Cover ends

Cut two ends from foam-core board. If you prefer that the cake is totally edible, you can form these ends from gum paste or pastillage. Cover both of the ends with frosting and mark the boards with a table knife. Brush with the same color as the box. Attach the ends to the box with a spoonful of buttercream.

Mark ends with knife

Position ends on box

70

Paint dowel for handle

Brush the dowel rod handle with brown liquid food color.

Arrange the tools in and around the box.

Insert the painted dowel rod into the hole in one end of the foam end and push through until it goes through the hole in the other end.

Box without handle

Inserting dowel handle

Close-up of tools

Chapter 5
Holidays

Blue Christmas

Holidays are special occasions that span the age spectrum. A special cake can put a twinkle in the eye of observers of all ages, whether it is an elegant Christmas occasion, a whimsical witch for Halloween, or an elf for St. Patrick's Day. The three cakes in this chapter use various techniques including gum paste snowflakes, wafer paper flowers, cone sculptors, and a gum ball elf.

Supplies
- 2 cake layers, 2-inch x 2-inch x 8-inch
- Poinsettia leaf pattern (see in Pattern section)
- 12-inch cake board
- 1 sheet wafer paper
- Piping gel
- Edible glitter
- One corsage pin
- Scissors
- One off-set spatula
- Flower former
- #3 decorator tip
- 1 cup royal frosting
- 1 decorator bag
- Rock candy
- Buttercream frosting, light blue and white
- Eatable Spray Lacquer
- Snowflake cutter/mold (Nick Lodge)
- Small ball white gum paste

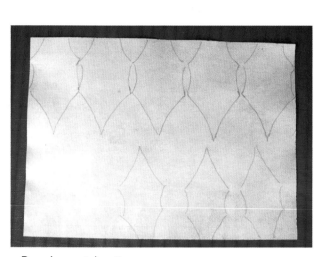

Drawing petal pattern

Spreading piping gel

Adding glitter

Using the leaf patterns found at the end of this book, draw five small, five medium, and five large petals on a sheet of wafer paper. Arrange the leaves to get all fifteen on one sheet.

With an off-set spatula, cover the entire sheet with piping gel. Remove all excess gel so only a light glaze remains.

Generously sprinkle the sheet with edible glitter. Gently raise the sheet and shake off any excess glitter to save for future use.

Allow the leaf sheet to dry from thirty minutes to an hour before cutting the leaves from the page. Do not allow the page to thoroughly dry as the sheet will become brittle, causing the leaves to break. If you have drawn the leaf outlines with a pencil, be sure to cut away all of these marks with the scissors. Lay the damp leaves in a flower former to slightly curve. The leaves should not be totally flat, but do not allow them to dry with too much curve.

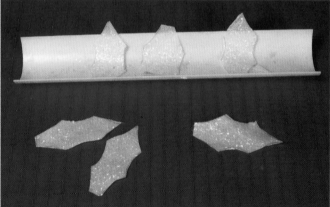

Place in former

Vein petals

Outline edges

Place white royal frosting in a decorator bag with tip #3. Pipe one long vein the length of the leaf and three or four smaller veins to the side edges of the leaf.

Outline the entire leaf edge with the royal and allow it to dry slightly curved. When the royal trim dries, the leaf will remain in that position.

Cut a 14-inch strip of aluminum foil and fold it in half lengthwise. Fold the width in half and crinkle the edges to form a cup-shaped circle that is 4 inches in diameter. This will be the drying form for the poinsettia. Cut a 2-inch diameter x 1/8-inch thick circle from white fondant and allow it to dry. Lay the dried circle into the aluminum foil cup as a base for the flower.

Form aluminum support

Flower base

First row of petals

Place a spoon full of royal frosting on the base that you have placed in the aluminum foil cup. Arrange the five largest petals in a circle. Space the petals equally and be sure that the ends are secure in the royal frosting. Add another spoon of royal in the center and arrange the medium petals for the second row of petals. Place the medium petals between the large petals.

Add another spoon of royal in the center and arrange the five small petals between the medium leaves.

Three rows of petals

Place a spoon of royal frosting in the center and cover the center with crushed or small pieces of rock candy to give the appearance of crystals. A few fondant pearls can be added for additional detail if desired.

Rock candy center

Snow at base of cake

Rather than the traditional tube border, the board and border area are covered with mounds of white buttercream. Use a spatula to swirl and blend the snow up on the sides of the cake to resemble drifted snow.

Snowflake mold

Delicate snowflakes are the perfect touch for a winter holiday cake. Roll a small piece of white gum paste very thin. Let the paste dry for a few seconds. Rather than cutting the paste by pushing the cutter against the paste on the table, it may be more effective to place the piece of gum paste over the cutter and press the intricate pattern with your thumb. Press away the excess paste around the edges.

Snowflake steps

Use a corsage pin to loosen the points and crevices of the snow flake. Do not force the snow flake to come out or it will tear. Gently loosen and allow the snowflake to fall gently on the table top. Remove any cutouts that remain with the corsage pin. Allow the snowflake to dry. Spray it lightly with eatable spray lacquer and sprinkle it generously with glitter.

Allow the snowflake to dry before attaching it to the cake side with a touch of royal frosting.

Close-up of snowflake

Place the completed poinsettia in the center of the cake top and lightly adhere with royal frosting. Arrange the snowflakes around the sides and sprinkle the entire cake with eatable glitter.

Close-up of poinsettia

Witches Brew

This simple little witch can be made days in advance to lessen the last minute work load. Candy corn simplifies the borders and any inscription can be added to personalize the event.

Supplies
- 2 cake layers, 2-inch x 2-inch x 8-inch inch cake
- Orange frosting
- Royal frosting – black and orange
- 2 cup ice cream cones
- 1 pointed ice cream cone
- Moss green dusting powder
- Paper towel
- 1 Tootsie Pop® sucker
- 1 piece heavy spaghetti uncooked
- 1 large gum ball
- 1/4 pound fondant
- 1/2 pound candy corn

Stack the two cup cones – one on top of the other and secure with royal frosting.

Generously frost the stacked cups with black royal frosting for the witches dress. When the frosting begins to air dry, use a paper towel to smooth and press vertical folds in the dress.

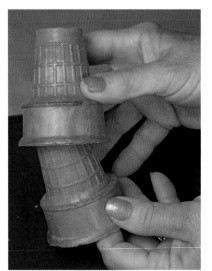

Stacking cones

Frosting cones

Forming head

Roll a ball of white fondant, about twice the size of the sucker you are using for the head, until smooth. Press the sucker firmly into the ball and work the fondant over the sucker until it is smooth. Trim any excess at the neck or sucker stick area. Shape the chin to a long sharp point. The hooked nose is formed from a small ball of fondant and added to the face with a touch of dampness. Press a hole between the nose and chin for the mouth.

Allow the head to dry then brush the face with moss green dusting powder.

Coloring face

Forming hat brim

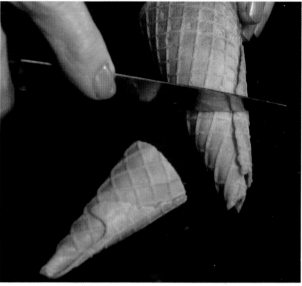
Cutting cone for hat

Roll a thin circle of black fondant or gum paste. Cut a 2-inch circle. Thin the edges between your thumb and forefinger and drape the piece over the witches head to shape and dry.

Measure 2-1/2 inches from the tip of the pointed ice cream cone and gently cut through the cone with a serrated knife and a gentle, sawing motion. Remove the pointed end and discard the remainder of the cone.

Frost the point with black royal frosting, smooth with a paper towel and set it aside to dry. When the point is dry enough to handle, attach it to the brim with black royal frosting.

Frosting hat

Roll two balls of green fondant that are equal in size. Cover one ball to prevent drying. To form the hand, roll the ball until it is smooth then elongate it into an oval. Mark the wrist area and flatten the hand. Cut a "V" shaped section to separate the thumb from the fingers. Snip three more cuts to separate the remaining fingers. Roll the tiny fingers between yours to thin them. Witches fingers should be extra long and skinny. Avoid having the hands in a straight, stiff position. Separate the fingers and shape them into a more natural position.

Forming hands

Painting fingernails

Forming sleeves

Inserting hand in sleeve

Roll a thin piece of black fondant that is approximately 2 inches in diameter. Cut a sleeve-shape piece, lift it and roll the sleeve around your forefinger. Dampen the seam to secure the connection. Thin the lower large opening between your thumb and forefinger and stretch it to lengthen one side of the lower sleeve. Add the sleeve to the dress with black royal. Allow the top edge to fold over the top of the cup cone.

Insert the hands into the lower part of the sleeve and secure them with royal frosting. The fingernails can be painted with food color for added detail.

Adding head

Painting eyes

Piping hair

Push the sucker stick of the head firmly into the top of the cup cone until it goes through both cones. Secure the head in place with royal frosting.

Paint the inside of the mouth with red food color. Paint two dots for the eyes with a black food writer pen or black food coloring on a tiny brush.

Pipe long straight strands of orange royal frosting hair with a #3 decorator tip. Place the completed hat onto the wet hair to secure it and add an orange hatband with the same #3 tip in a short up/down motion.

Forming broom handle

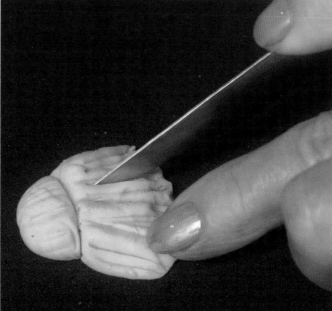

Forming broom

Break a piece of heavy spaghetti to a length of 7 inches. Cover the spaghetti with brown tinted fondant.

Blend a marble size piece of yellow and brown fondant to resemble the color of a broom. Smooth the piece and form into a flat wedge shape. Insert the handle and use a dull knife to form broom straws with many tiny marks.

Witches pot

Close up of witches pot

To create the witches pot, cover a large gum ball with black fondant. Pinch a rim around the top edge with your fingers. Roll a narrow black rope and form a small circle to set the pot onto as a base.

Place some white frosting in the opening of the pot and scatter some small fondant pearls on top. Brush the contents of the pot with silver luster or gray dusting powder to create an ere appearance. Cover a 2-inch piece of spaghetti with the same brown fondant as the broom handle and insert into the pot. To create a fire under the pot, pipe short flames with the #3 tip and orange royal. Brush portions of the flames with red to create a more realistic fire. Short pieces of brown fondant or pieces of a Tootsie Roll form the wood in the fire.

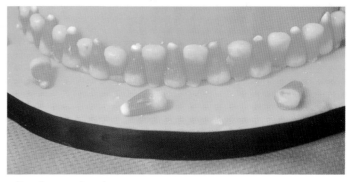

Candy corn borders

Pot of Gold

Everyone dreams of finding a pot of gold at the end of the rainbow so this cake, covered with golden coins, is watchfully protected by a sly little gum ball leprechaun.

Supplies
- 2-quart aluminum or Pyrex baking bowl
- 1/2 pound gold candy coins
- 1 sucker
- 1 medium gum ball
- 6 cookies
- Frosting, black, brown
- 1 pound fondant
- Serrated knife
- Food color pen
- Small blossom cutter

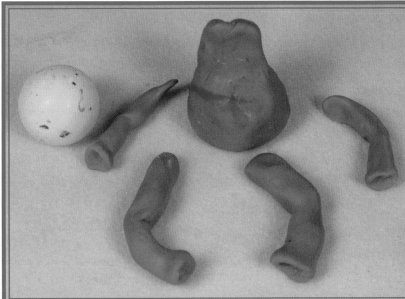

Leprechaun body parts

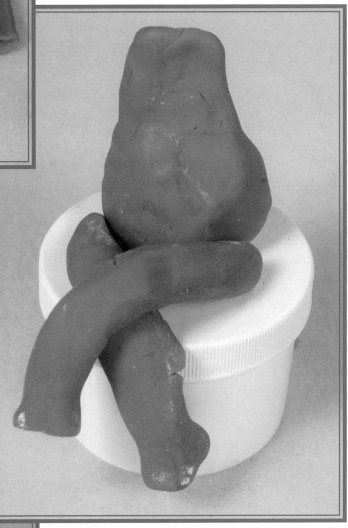

Shaping legs to dry

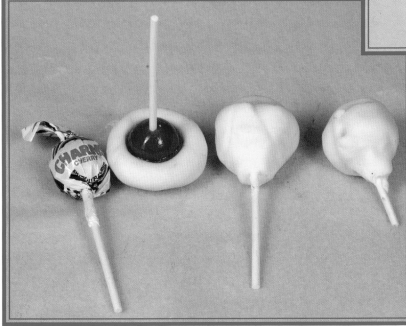

Shaping head

Using green fondant, mold the leprechaun with the same procedure used in making the clown.

Because the leprechaun will be in a sitting position, the legs need to be dried on something compatible to the stump such as a piping gel container.

To form the head, place a ball of flesh color fondant in the palm of your hand and press a sucker firmly into the paste. Follow the instructions given to form the witch's head in the previous cake directions.

Shoes for the figure should be pointed and curled up on the ends to look like pixie shoes. Roll a ball of green fondant about the size of a walnut until it is smooth. Pinch up a small area for the ankle that will be inserted into the leg of the pants. Elongate the remainder of the ball and flatten. Use a small skewer to press up under the instep of the shoes, emphasizing the heel. Use the same skewer to roll the toe of the shoe back towards the shoe. Remove the skewer to leave a curl on the toe of the shoe.

The hat is also a pixie design. Start with a large walnut-shaped green ball. Roll the ball until it is smooth and elongated to a point. Flatten the bottom. Mold the flat area over the rounded part of the pre-formed head. Bend the point to the side of the hat.

Shaping pixie shoes

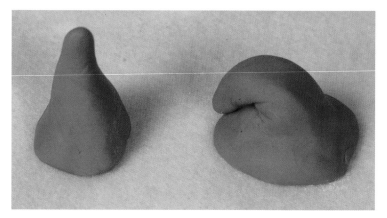

Forming hat

Stacking cookies for stump

To form the stump, begin with six medium size cookies such as sugar or oatmeal cookies. Stack the cookies, adding frosting between each cookie to secure them.

Frost the entire stack of cookies leaving the frosting rough to resemble bark. After you place it on the board, pull out some areas of frosting to replicate roots of the stump.

Frosting cookie stump

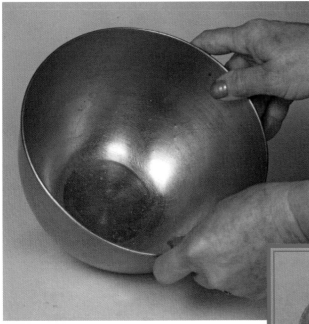

Baking bowl

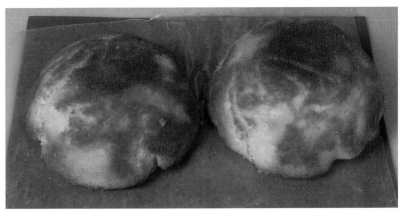

Cakes for leprechaun pot

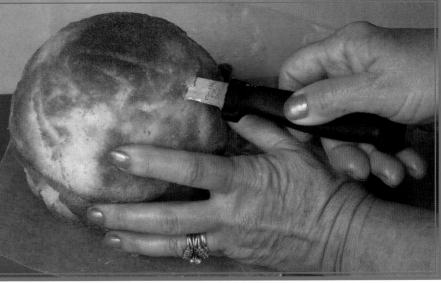

Cutting top of pot

The pictured cake was baked in a two quart aluminum mixing bowl, but a Pyrex bowl or a ball pan will achieve the same results.

Fill and bake the bowl twice to form two ball halves. Frost the two halves together.

Use the serrated knife to slice about 1/2-inch from the top to form a flat area. Frost the entire cake with black buttercream.

Frosting pot black

Forming ring for top of pot

Remove ring from bowl

Placing ring on pot

Use a small dome shaped bowl as a mold to create the lip or flange for the top of the pot. Cut a 1-1/2-inch strip of black fondant. Cover the bowl with clear plastic wrap to prevent sticking and wrap the black fondant strip around the mold. Allow the wide part of the fondant to rest on the countertop. Trim the end and secure it to form a ring. Press the top part of the ring against the narrow part of the bowl and allow it to dry.

Gently remove the ring from the mold and remove the plastic wrap.

Place the narrow part of the ring against the top of the cake so the ring flares out at the top.

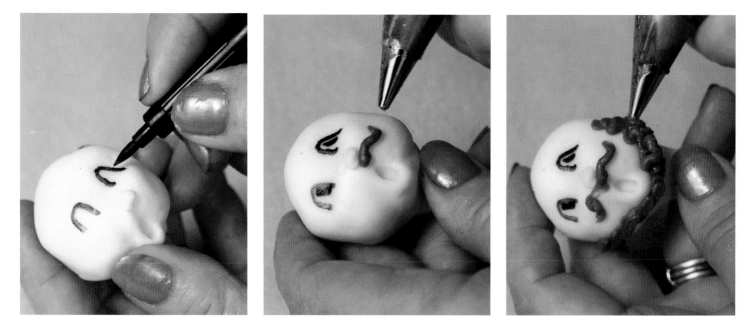

Adding eyes to leprechaun

Adding mustache

Adding beard

Outline and add a pupil to the eyes with a black food safe pen.

Place brown frosting and a # 2 or 3 decorator tip into a decorator bag. Pipe a single curved line under each side of the nose for the mustache.

Insert the head into the body of the leprechaun and with a circular motion, add the beard and hair. Place the pixie hat onto the wet hair. Use a #14 star tip and add a lighter green trim to the neck, front, sleeves and cuffs of the leprechaun suit. Green candies can be added for buttons.

Tiny flowers

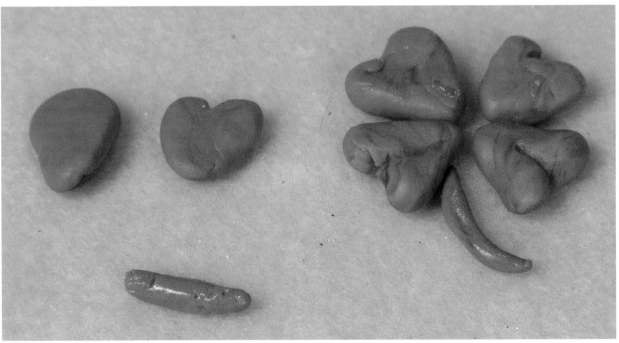

Forming shamrocks

Use a tiny flower cutter and cut blossoms from various colors thin gum paste. Indent the flowers and place a center in each.

Form the shamrocks by arranging four small green hearts with the points to the center. These can be piped with green buttercream or cut with a tiny heart shaped cutter from green gum paste.

Chapter 6

The Golden Years

• • • • • • • • •

Gone Fishing

As we celebrate all of the occasions of a life time the "Golden Years" are brought to our attention. These special years are labeled as such because after a lifetime of work and raising family, the retirement years are set aside to reap the rewards of a lifetime. They should be a time to travel, golf, fish, and to enjoy all of our favorite hobbies.

Supplies
- 3 layers baked in oval pan, 9-inch x 2-inch
- 1/2 pound brown colored fondant
- Oval cake board approximately 14-inch x 18-inch
- 1 purchased fish stringer
- 2 batches pastillage
- Serrated knife
- Decorator tips, #10 and #12
- Tan buttercream frosting
- Dusting powder colors, green, pink, gray
- Black liquid food color
- Small paint brushes
- Brown sugar or raw granulated sugar
- 1 pound white chocolate
- Fishing tools candy mold (CK Products)

Bake, cool, stack, and frost the three cake layers. Use a serrated knife to trim the creel to shape. It should taper in at the top and bottom and round in the center. Trim the back so that it is flat or straight up and down. Lightly crumb coat the entire cake. Cut a 2-inch x 2-inch x 1-inch deep square from the top of the lid to resemble the opening to place the fish inside the creel.

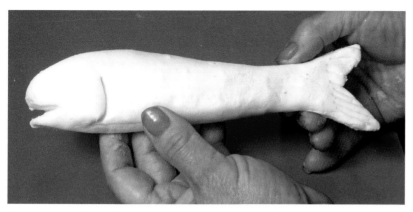
Forming pastillage fish

Coloring dried fish

To form the fish, kneed pre-made pastillage until it is smooth, then hand mold the body of a fish that is approximately 9 inches long. Flatten the tail fin and mark lines with a table knife. Form the half fish with the tail to insert into the top of the creel. Allow the fish to dry overnight before moving.

Brush the top half of the fish with dark green dusting powder. Add a pink line horizontally down the center and brush the stomach area with silver or gray.

Dip a tiny brush into the black liquid food color and add black dots across the fish back and center to get the effect of a trout.

Speckles on fish

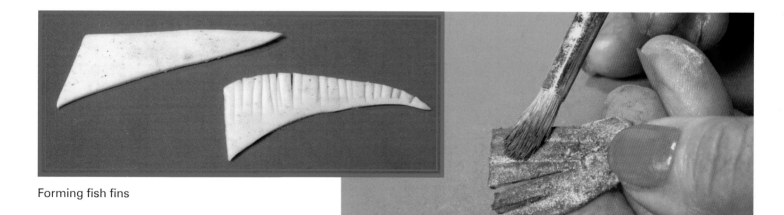
Forming fish fins

Roll a thin piece of white pastillage and cut the fins. Use a knife to score the lines in each piece to resemble fins.

When the pieces are dry, brush each with dusting powder and attach them to the fish with royal frosting.

Painting fins

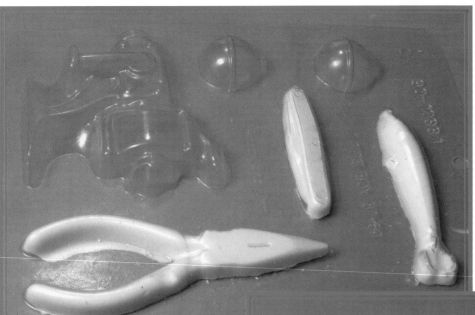

Molding tools

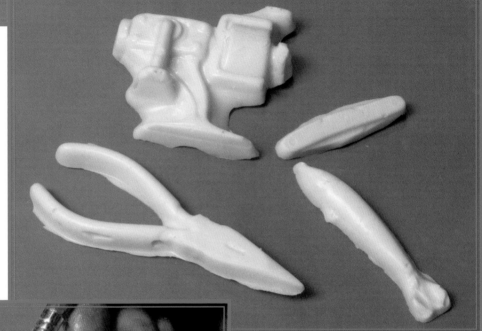

Unmolding tools

Painting tools

Melt white chocolate and fill the candy mold cavities to form the fishing tools. Refrigerate the candy until the chocolate is hard.

Invert the mold and tap lightly to remove the pieces. Trim the excess candy from each piece with a sharp knife.

Color the candy tools with dry dusting powder in the colors of your choice.

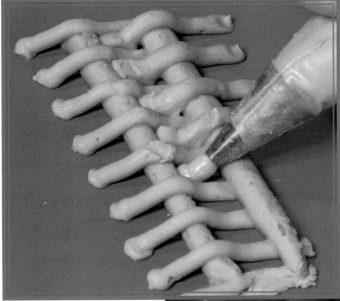

Basket weave pattern

The cake is covered in basket weave to represent a wicker creel. Using a #12 decorator tip and tan frosting, start at the top edge of the basket and pipe a straight line vertically to the base of the basket. With a smaller #10 decorator tip, pipe horizontal lines across the vertical line leaving a space less than 1/4 inch to allow space for the next row of horizontal lines. Use the #12 tip to pipe a second vertical line over the ends of the horizontal lines.

Repeat this process until the cake sides and top are completely covered.

Basket weave on cake

To form the rope edging around the edge of the lid, roll two long narrow pieces of brown fondant and twist the two together. Secure the rope around the edge of the creel with frosting. Repeat the rope process to outline the hole in the lid.

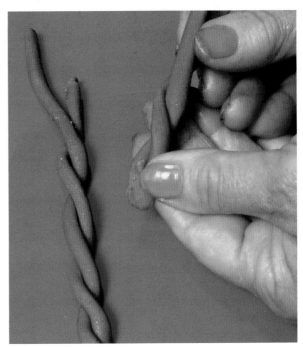

Fondant rope trim

Fish beside basket

Fish inserted in lid

Generously sprinkle the raw sugar or brown sugar to resemble sand on the cake board. Arrange the large fish and chocolate tools at the base of the creel in the sand.

Insert the half fish into the hole of the lid.

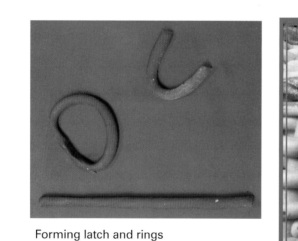

Forming latch and rings

Basket strap & latch

Cut 1-1/2-inch strips of brown fondant for the straps that hold the fastener and handle. Arrange the straps on the creel while they are damp and pliable so they will conform to the shape of the cake. The rings and catch are formed from thin rolls of brown fondant that are shaped then allowed to dry. Cut a long 1-1/2-inch x 16-inch strip for the shoulder strap. Secure the strap on either end of the creel and allow it to drape naturally at the base of the creel.

Golden Anniversary

One of the greatest milestones that a married couple can reach is that of their Golden or 50th Anniversary. My husband and I had the privilege of reaching this special event on June 2. To commemorate the occasion, I would like to share this special cake featuring photographs of Bill and I on the top layer; our three children, Gina, Bret, and Lori on the center tier and our four grandchildren from left to right, Hunter, Bretani, Collan, and Wesley on the bottom layer. The Golden Anniversary is certainly a celebratory occasion to be portrayed in cake and a fitting event with which to conclude this book. Thank you for sharing this important occasion with my family.

Supplies
- Three cake tiers, 16-inch x 4-inch, 12-inch x 4-inch, and 10-inch x 4-inch
- One cake tier, 6-inch x 3-inch
- Gold colored pearls
- Diamond embossing sheet
- Embossing roller
- White buttercream
- 18-inch cake board
- #3 decorating tip
- Decorating bag
- Edible image photographs
- 1 pound fondant
- Piping gel
- Gum paste cutters for rose, lily and calla lily
- Ball tool
- Cel pad
- Off-set spatula
- #30 floral wire
- Gold dusting powder
- Floral tape
- Royal frosting
- 50th Anniversary cake topper

Prepare the tiered cake with supports as per directions for "Something Blue" in Chapter 4. Frost around the edge of the board and finish the edge by gluing a gold ribbon around the edge of the board.

To prepare the pictures select appropriate size snapshots and enlarge or reduce on a printer until they are equal size. Arrange the photos on a sheet of white paper and take them to a cake shop that will make an edible copy of your photos for a small fee.

Edible image sheet

Create the picture frames allowing sufficient time for drying before they are placed on the cake. Roll out a small piece of pastillage or fondant. There are oval scalloped frames available for purchase, but if you do not have one, you can improvise. Cut the frames with a round cutter. Use a size smaller circle and cut out the center of the first circle. This will leave a circle that is approximately 1/4 inch. Gently stretch the circle to form the necessary size oval.

Forming picture frames

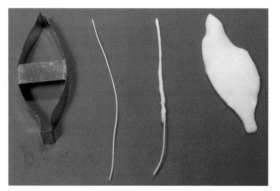

Cutting lily petal

Veining lily petal

To make Golden Lilies, cut six pieces of #30 gauge wire, approximately 3 inches long to form center veins in the petals for each lily. Roll a tiny ball of fresh white gumpaste around the wire. Cover the area that will be inside the petal by rolling it between your fingers. Make certain that the top end of the wire is covered. Do not cover the exposed stem area of the wire. Repeat this process for all six wires and cover them with plastic to prevent drying.

To form the petals, roll out white paste moderately thin and cut six petals. Place one petal into the bottom piece of a lily veiner. Lay a prepared wire onto the petal, making sure it is in the center and reaches almost to the tip of the leaf. The exposed wire will extend from the mold for the stem. Place the top half of the mold over the covered wire and press very firmly.

Remove the veined petal from the mold; the wire should be firmly impressed into the leaf. Lay the petal on a cell pad and soften the edges with a ball tool. Petals can be bent or curved at this point and allowed to dry. When the petals are dry, brush with pearl luster and highlight the edges with gold and paint scattered gold speckles on the leaves.

Shaping and painting lily petal

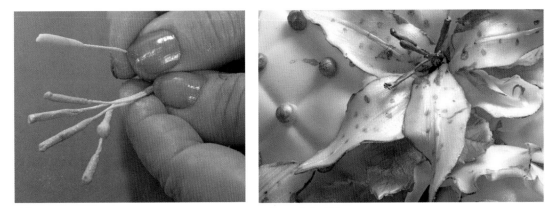

Lily stamens   Completed lily

For each lily, cut six stamens from #30 white fabric covered wire. Roll a tiny ball of white paste into a bead and cover the end of each wire. Place the six stamens together and secure with floral tape. Dip the cluster into gold luster dust.

Arrange three dried petals around the golden stamens. Add three more petals between the first three then tape the stems to hold in place.

Cutting and shaping calla lily

Coloring dried calla

Inserting stamen in calla

For Calla Lilies, roll white paste thinly and cut flowers with a calla lily cutter or template (The pictured cutter is a "Q" shaped cookie cutter that has been bent to shape).

Lay a petal on the cel pad and soften the upper half of the flowers with a ball tool. Roll the base of the blossom around a small, pointed, paper drinking cup to use as a drying support and secure the connection with a drop of water or gum glue. Roll the side edges with your fingertips to give the flower a more realistic shape. Allow the flowers to remain on the cups until firm then remove to complete the drying process.

Brush the throat of the flower with light green dusting power then dust the entire lily with pearl luster. Add a fine line of gold luster around the edge.

For the centers, roll a small log of paste with white or yellow. Brush the stamen with gold luster and let dry. Insert the center into the throat of the lily and secure it with a small dot of royal frosting.

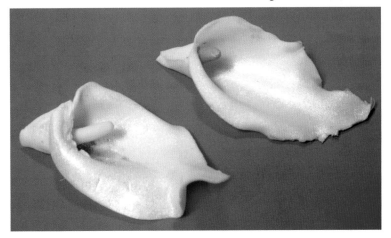

Completed calla

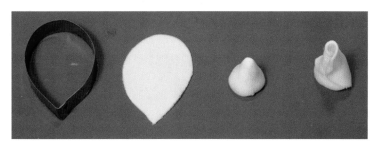

Cutting rose petal

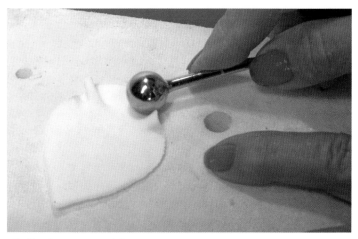

Softening rose petal

Shaping rose petals

To create roses, form the center by making a small cone shape from the fondant or other paste that you are using. Large roses need a large cone and smaller roses need a small cone.

Roll a thin piece of paste and cut three petals. Brush the lower half of each with vodka. Wrap the first petal around the top of the cone. It will extend above the top of the core. Add the second and third petal, overlapping each slightly. These petals do not have as much curl as the outer petals. Cut five more petals for a medium size rose.

Soften the top edge of each petal with a ball tool. Lay each petal into the length of a plastic soup spoon and roll the top edge to shape and curl (Soup spoons have a larger bowl than a teaspoon so they give a better cup shape to the petal). Sit aside to dry. Cut seven additional petals and place in the spoons to form a large rose. Depending on the humidity in your area the petals will need to dry two hours to overnight. Remove the petals from the spoons and brush with pearl luster and outline the petal edges with gold luster.

The flower formers are made from strips of aluminum foil. Cut a strip 4-6 inches wide and fold in half to form a square. Crush the edges and mold into a circular cup shape. To form the medium size rose, select five dried petals and place a dot of royal frosting on the lower edge of each. Place the first petal against a cone that has the three petals already arranged. Slip the second petal slightly inside the first and continue the arrangement until the five petals surround the cone. Set the rose inside the foil former and position the foil to hold the petals in place until the royal dries them securely. To form a larger rose, remove the medium rose from the foil and add seven additional petals using the same method and place in the former again to complete the drying.

Completed rose and calla

Rose leaf

Cut white leaves with a rose leaf cutter. The pictured cutter also incorporates the veins. Lay the leaves in a flower former to curve. When the leaves are dry, paint them with gold luster dust.

Emboss the second and top tier with a diamond shape embosser sheet. Lay the plastic sheet slightly against the side of the cake and press firmly to push the raised pattern into the frosting so that it will leave a visible diamond impression. It is necessary to line up the design and overlap the pattern slightly to have a continuous pattern around the cake.

Add a small dot of frosting where each lines crosses and attach a gold pearl at the center of each. Continue the pattern around the cake. The pearls are cut and formed as described in chapter 4. To coat with gold luster dust, drop the beads into a small jar which has a lid and add dry luster. The amount of luster will depend on how many pearls you intend to make. I keep jars with various colors of luster dust specifically for pearls. Shake the jar vigorously to coat all of the pearls.

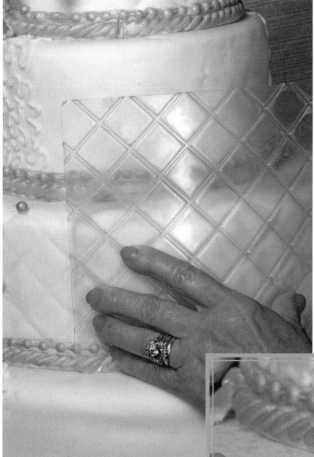

Embossing diamond pattern

Placing gold pearls on design

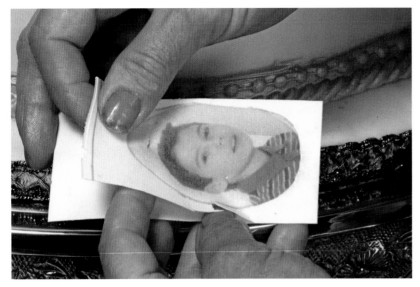

Removing edible image picture

Applying piping gel to cake

Arranging edible image on cake

Cut and trim an oval edible image photograph from the sheet and gently remove the backing from the picture.

Spread a light coat of piping gel on the area of the cake where the photo will be attached. Remove any excess with an offset spatula.

Gently position the picture on the side of the cake. These images are very fragile so handle them with care.

Placing frame around photo

Select one of the pre-dried gold frames and pipe a thin line of frosting on the back side of it. Place the frame over the photo. The line of frosting adheres it to the cake.

The arrangement of photographs places the anniversary couple on the upper layer, the children on the middle layer and the grandchildren on the base layer. If great grandchildren are included, each generation can be moved up one layer.

Placement of edible images

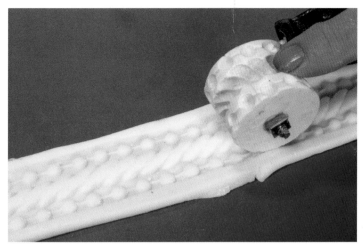

Impression roller on border

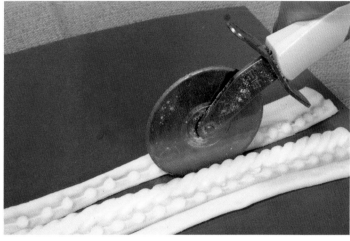

Trimming border

To form the borders, roll a long strip of fondant that is a medium thickness. Use an impression roller to emboss the rope and pearl border design. If you do not have a distinct impression, your fondant may be too thin.

With a pizza cutter trim away one row of pearls and closely trim against the top row of pearls. To prevent the rope from stretching, cut narrow strips of plastic wrap (2-3 inches). Lay the strips over the rope and roll up the border so that you can hold it on one hand and apply it to the cake with the other.

The border will adhere better if you first pipe a line of frosting onto the cake. Mix gold luster powder and vodka to liquefy the luster and paint the borders.

Completed border

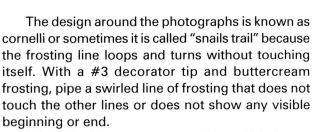

Piping cornelli design on cake

The design around the photographs is known as cornelli or sometimes it is called "snails trail" because the frosting line loops and turns without touching itself. With a #3 decorator tip and buttercream frosting, pipe a swirled line of frosting that does not touch the other lines or does not show any visible beginning or end.

Fill in all of the space around the edible image photographs on the first and third layers.

Cornelli design around photos

Arrangement of sugar flowers

Place a mound of frosting on top of the cake and arrange the pre-dried flowers on the top layer and cascade them over the top and down the side of the second layer. Place an individual lily on the top side of the bottom layer. Insert a purchased golden 50 ornament into the top of the arrangement.

Floral placement

Golden 50 top piece

Chapter 7

Patterns

● ● ● ● ● ● ● ●

Special Delivery

Brontosaurus

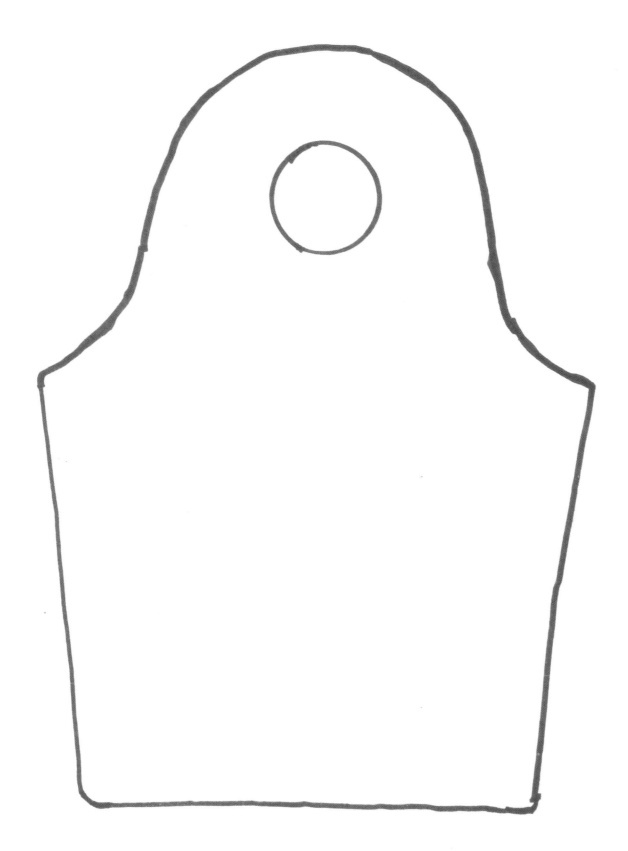

Blue Christmas

Gone Fishing

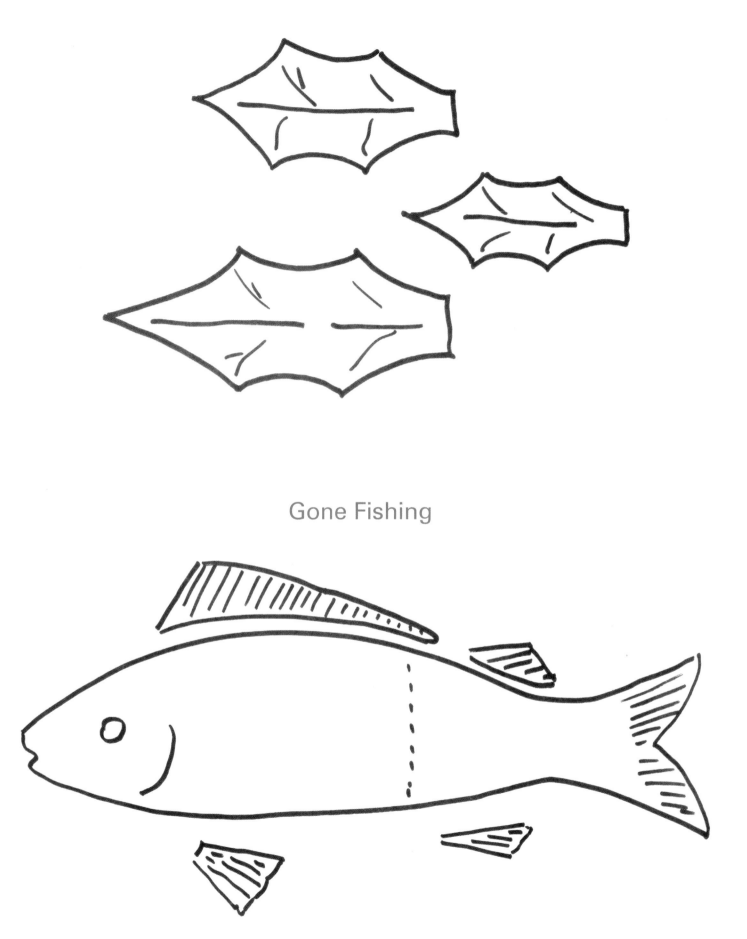

Glossary of Terms

Ameri-Color Gourmet Food Pen: Available in a colorful set, these pens look like felt-tip markers, but they are filled with food color.

ball tool: A plastic, stainless steel or Plexiglas instrument with a small ball on each end of the tool; used to thin, soften or ruffle sugar flower petals.

ball pan: An interlocking, two-piece pan that forms a 6-inch round ball cake.

blossom cutter: A plastic or metal tool used to cut a variety of flower blossoms from gum paste or fondant

buttercream: An all-purpose decorating frosting made from a base of powdered sugar, shortening and flavorings. This frosting is widely used in the United States.

cel pad: A small piece of a specially formulated, dense foam used in the formation of thinning sugar petals.

Chocopan: A specially formulated blend of fondant and white chocolate developed by Linda Shonk of Indianapolis, IN, that rolls into a plastic smooth surface and tastes delectable.

clay gun: A small cylindrical tool. A small amount of fondant is placed inside the cylinder and pressed through a variety of patterned disk to form numerous designs.

crumb coat: A thin coating of buttercream frosting spread on the cake layers to seal the cake. When this covering dries it prevents crumbs from accumulating in the finished layer of frosting.

dusting colors: Powdered food colors used to color and accent sugar flowers and decorations. U.S.D.A. Food Approved colors can be obtained from Beth Parvu of Indiana.

edible glitter: This substance looks like real glitter on the cake, but it is actually dried flakes of gum arabic.

embossed roller: Rolling pins in assorted shapes and sizes with various designs etched into the roller. These patterns transfer onto the fondant when firmly pressed over it.

floral tape: A stretchy, paper tape used to cover wires and connect flowers and sprays. It is available in shades of green, brown and white.

gum glue: A mixture of powdered gum arabic and water used to connect two pieces of damp gum paste.

gum paste: A pliable, elastic dough using the basic ingredient of gum tragacanth. Gum paste is the principal substance used in the formation of sugar flowers.

impression mats: Plastic sections molded with various designs that transfer onto rolled fondant or sugar paste when pressed into the paste. Some of these transfers will also work with buttercream frosting such as the diamond impression mat.

luster dust: Colored powders with a high sheen or gloss. Pearl, gold, silver and bronze are luster dusts that are qualified as non-toxic but are not currently certified by the U.S.D.A. as food safe color. Use with caution.

pastillage: Depending on the recipe, pastillage is a cooked or uncooked sugar paste. The cooked variety is made from granulated sugar, water, and gelatin blended with powdered sugar to form thick sugar dough used in the formation of sugar buildings and figurines. The uncooked variety was used on the fish in Chapter 6. Pastillage is less expensive than gum paste and it dries quickly and hard.

piping gel: A transparent gel that can be tinted various colors.

ribbon cutter: Two rolling blades connected at an established parallel to cut strips of sugar paste to form ribbon loops and stripes.

rolled buttercream: A dough-like frosting with the basic ingredients of buttercream than can be rolled between sheets of plastic to resemble "fake" fondant.

royal frosting: A smooth, hard-drying frosting made from meringue powder (pasteurized dried egg whites).

textured rolling pin: Beautiful acrylic rolling pins with carved or laser cut designs to create perfect patterns when rolled over fondant.

tylose: A powder used as a binder and thickener in sugar paste and fondant.

unflavored gelatin: An ingredient used in gum paste and pastillage to thicken the paste. The powder is used like gelatin but has no flavoring.

wafer paper: Sheets of rice paper that can be eaten. Designs can be traced through this paper with food color pens. It is great for butterflies and accent pieces.

Recipes

Buttercream Frosting

- 3 cups Crisco® shortening
- 1/4 teaspoon salt
- 2 tablespoons flavoring of you choice
- 1/4 cup water
- 4 pounds powdered sugar

Mix all ingredients until thick and creamy

Flower Paste

- 1 pound purchased fondant
- 2 teaspoons tylose powder

Mix and blend the powder into the fondant. Wrap the dough in plastic wrap and store in a plastic bag. Allow the mixture to cure at least overnight. Use this mixture for sugar paste flowers or where you would use gum paste.

Edible Glitter

To make edible glitter, brush a very thin coat of gum glue onto a piece of glass and let it dry in the oven with only the oven light turned on. When it is dry it will peel away from the glass and it can be scraped off and crushed into very fine glitter. This glitter can be tinted any color by adding food color to the gum glue. This can also be painted inside a Pyrex bowl. Pour the glitter between two sheets of waxed paper and roll with a rolling pin until it is very fine. Store the glitter in a tight container to preserve.

Gum Glue

- 1 teaspoon gum arabic
- 3 teaspoons water

Mix the powdered gum arabic with the water and let sit until it thickens to the consistency of glue. You can use this to paint on fresh gum paste in order to stick two pieces together. When this mixture is painted on dry pieces, it will shine like varnish.

Gum Paste

- 2 cups powdered sugar
- 1 tablespoon gum tragacanth
- 1 ball glucose about the size of a walnut
- 2 tablespoons warm water

Mix the powdered sugar and the gum tragacanth. Form a hole in the center and add the glucose and warm water. Work until the mixture becomes pliable. If it is too sticky, add more powdered sugar. If it is dry and does not knead well, add a few drops of water. Wrap your gum paste in plastic wrap or a plastic bag and store in an airtight container.

Royal Frosting With Egg Whites

- 2 egg whites
- 1/2 teaspoon cream of tartar
- Approximately 1 pound of powdered sugar

Beat the egg whites to a foamy stage. Add the cream of tartar and enough powdered sugar to beat the mixture into a stiff icing. If the icing gets too thick, it can be thinned with a little lemon juice. Store the frosting in an airtight container after each use. Because of health regulations with uncooked eggs, this frosting should be used for decorative purposes only and not for consumption.

Royal Frosting With Meringue Powder

- 3 tablespoons Meringue Powder
- 6 tablespoons water
- Approximately 1 pound of powdered sugar

Beat all ingredients until the icing forms peaks. Store in an air tight container.

Pastillage – Cooked

- 1 tablespoon unflavored gelatin
- 2/3 cup granulated sugar
- 2 pounds powdered sugar
- 1/2 cup water to dampen sugar
- 1/2 cup water to dampen gelatin

In a heavy pot that has an even distribution of heat, place the granulated sugar and 1/2 cup of water. Stir the mixture to blend. Place the pot on the stove and bring the mixture to a soft boil stage without stirring. Pour the syrup into the dissolved gelatin and stir. Place just enough powdered sugar into the syrup and stir until the mixture looks like thick cream. Cover the mixture with an air tight lid and set aside until it cools thoroughly – at least overnight. When you are ready to use the pastillage, remove a small amount and work with powdered sugar until it is smooth and pliable. Keep the mixture covered as it dries quickly.

Pastillage – Uncooked

- 1 pound powdered sugar
- 3 tablespoons water
- 2 tablespoons lemon juice
- 1 envelope unflavored gelatin (1 tablespoon)
- 1 heaping teaspoon glucose (do not substitute corn syrup)

Mix water, lemon juice, and gelatin in the top of a double boiler and let sponge. Place the bowl over the warm water and add the glucose into the mixture and add the powdered sugar. You may need more sugar, but leave the mixture a little thin until it cools. Place clear plastic wrap over the pastillage and let it cool at least an hour and preferably overnight. When using, keep the excess covered as it will dry quickly.